☑ Check
☑ Mark
☐ Startup

A Step-By-Step Guide To

Starting Your Successful Business

RICHARD WAYNE BOBHOLZ

ISBN: 0-9977338-1-0
ISBN-13: 978-0-9977338-1-5

DEDICATION

For longer than I've been alive, there has been one person who has dedicated her life to making sure that mine is a happy, successful, meaningful life. Without my mother, this book wouldn't have happened and my life wouldn't be where it is right now.

As early as I can remember, my mom had me going to summer educational programs, studying with flashcards, learning about computers and more, all so that I could always be challenged academically. For those of you who do know me personally, I'm sure you can imagine what an independent child I was. (Independent is the nice choice of words).

Though there have been many times I didn't take her advice, I love receiving it (even if not at that exact moment) because if there's one person I know who is always putting my wellbeing first, it is her.

Thank you mom! I know I was a difficult child, but I appreciate everything you've done to get me to where I am today. Your love and compassion have fueled me to be a strong, independent, and compassionate person myself. Without all that you have provided, I could not imagine where I would be today. Throughout all my successes and struggles, it is amazing to know that you will be there for me.

Thank you.

CONTENTS

ACKNOWLEDGMENTS

So many people have helped make this book possible that listing them all would be a book itself. Generally, I would like to thank all those in the Raleigh-Durham small business community who have inspired me, all the reviewers that have given their feedback, and the editors, advisors and mentors I've had in this lengthy process.

A special thanks goes out to my friends and colleagues who helped me edit this book. As they are incredibly aware, I am not the best person at finding typos or those really weird formatting mistakes. Kristin Thompson, Eric Brei, Lee Heinrich, and Nicole Gross were all incredibly helpful in ensuring this book was more readable, followed a logical progression, and didn't have extremely long complicated sentences like this one. Unfortunately for you, they didn't help with this Acknowledgments section! If there are still typos remaining in the book, which I'm sure there are, please feel free to blame them. I am, of course, just kidding. I'm greatly appreciative of their time and talents in helping make this book into what it is today.

Additionally, I want to thank all my clients and colleagues who have helped me formulate these ideas over the past three years. Writing this book was no small feat. It took hundreds of hours, and as many conversations to develop the system upon which this book is built.

I'm a strong believer that an individual can be greater with the help of other great people, so I extend my thanks to all those who helped make this book a reality.

INTRODUCTION

If you want to create a strong business foundation upon which to build, this book is for you. This book is a step-by-step guide to starting a stable business with a great legal foundation, and is meant to help businesses grow with minimal setbacks. The purpose behind writing this is to give those starting a business a step-by-step guide to creating a business right the first time while being conscious of cost, time constraints and individual values. Your business's chance of success will greatly increase and you will avoid many of the growing pains most startups face by following this guide.

Why Listen to Me?

As I am writing this, I am 28-years-old, have been an attorney for only three years, and am entering into a field of authors who have several decades more experience than I do. Why would you ever consider my advice? Don't. At least don't blindly follow what I, or what anyone, say for that matter. Entrepreneurship is about gaining knowledge and experiences, not about following someone else's path. You'll see that this book is more about guiding you to give yourself the best advice than it is about getting answers from me.

As for what qualifies me to create the system described in this book, I have more experience in systems that almost any of my legal colleagues. I've been a computer programmer for longer than twenty years, and the thought processes involved in programming are ingrained in my everyday thinking. On top of that, I have a degree in Economics, where I was forced to evaluate the value of time and money in a free market system. During my studies, I had ample opportunity to evaluate how my values fit into a business setting.

I've also, at the time of writing this book, have started seven companies, all of which were successful in their own ways. No, I'm not a billionaire entrepreneur, but I've never had to struggle with being satisfied with my startup choices.

My highest personal values are liberty, honesty, and efficiency. You'll find that I incorporate those into every aspect of my life. I live these systems I'm providing you and because of them, I'm able to live a happy and productive life with a rock-solid foundation to build off of.

Law Plus Plus, the firm I founded, was established to change the legal system. We do that by applying scientific thought and mathematical analysis to every aspect of our operations. The end result: we're able to complete tasks that once took us hours in minutes. Tasks that took us weeks take us only a couple of hours now, and throughout all of it, we produce a better product because we have the systems in place to be able to do so.

Aside from Law Plus Plus, I've helped hundreds of other companies get started, and I have a stake in several of these companies myself.

These systems I've setup for you are merely the result of breaking every step of the creation process into finer, more manageable, details, and at that, I'm very good. I am neither an expert in every industry, nor do I have any idea how to best build your individual business. Those answers can be found in you and in the community.

Some books provide a system for setting up your company that has worked for many companies before. What I've found lacking in those books is the ability to create a custom system for yourself. What works in one business may not work in yours. Most of the business books I've read make an enormous number of assumptions about you and your wealth. I took great strides to not assume anything about you or your wealth in this book because I know nothing about you.

What I provide is a system to get to the answers you need. Any book that can provide you with specific answers is either lying to you, or is in such a specific niche that there are only few who can benefit. The world is constantly changing. The only thing that can remain static is a way of thinking about a changing world.

Put as nerdy as possible: I'm providing the derivative of the answers. This system exists only to provide you with the way of coming up with all the correct answers yourself, and I know you'll find the value in that idea.

How to Use this Book

This guide is not a cookie-cutter approach to starting a company, but rather a methodology of thinking that puts the business owner's values in the forefront and the concepts needed to build a company's foundation top of mind. These steps and the accompanying appendices and online material will be very useful in your startup process.

Every step is highlighted to stand out. Use this book, the margins, a notebook, or any other space to write down your answers. The value you get out of this book is found primarily in your answers. You'll find that the information you start accumulating is too much to keep unorganized, so I recommend an electronic system from the start.

Although this guide is geared toward someone new to the startup field, it should positively impact even the most seasoned entrepreneur. Because this guide breaks everything down into its core components, it will be easy for anyone of any skill level to follow. I ask that if you are a veteran, do not try to skip steps because each step is vital to creating the stable, value-driven company that will grow on a solid legal foundation.

Everything needed to start and run a successful business can be broken down into four categories: Production, Expansion, Protection and Administration.

- Production - Doing the work you already have to generate cash. This is the product or service you offer to your customers.
- Expansion - Generating more work to get more cash.
- Protection - Protecting the cash and work you already have.
- Administration - The necessary extra effort or value you must exert to complete any of the three previous categories.

If something cannot be classified into one of these four

categories, it is unnecessary as part of your business. Bear in mind that some things may be difficult to classify as one of the four categories, but the difficulty in which something is classified has very little bearing on whether or not it is an unnecessary activity.

Also note that administration items must be necessary. Otherwise, they should be excluded. The process of this book automatically excludes the unnecessary items from your business, and that is part of the true power of this book. We will refer to items in these categories throughout.

An example of an unnecessary item would be a purely social activity. If these activities do not yield an expansion, protection or production result, they have no place in the business. Many social functions, however, do yield expansion and protection results.

Comparative Advantage

It is a well-known fact that most entrepreneurs are really good at the one thing that makes their company stand out. For trades men and women, that's going to be their trade, like carpentry. For professionals and service providers, it will be the service they offer. Because the entrepreneur is great at one thing and other entrepreneurs around him or her are really good at other things, you can actually both benefit by providing the service to each other. This is a concept called comparative advantage.

Because of this concept, you shouldn't hesitate to get help from others. If that person is better or faster than you, or they're comparatively faster or better, they can benefit you and your company.

Here is an example to explain comparative advantage that I frequently heard while studying for my bachelors in economics: pizza and beer. If John can produce 12 pizzas an hour, or he can produce 6 beers per hour, and Sally can produce 8 pizzas or 5 beers per hour, they would both benefit if John produced only pizza and Sally produced only beer. That way, they could end up with 12 pizzas and 5 beers per hour. If John, who can produce beer faster than Sally, mixed it up and produced 8 pizzas and 2 beers, they would end up with a loss in efficiency, regardless of what Sally produced. By specializing, each party can gain overall through trade than if they just tried to produce the products on their own. Keep in mind that even if you're better at all items than someone else, they may be comparatively better.

In the real world, it comes down to an example more like this: Eric, an attorney billing $150/hour, has 60 hours to spend each week. If he spends 20 hours doing billable work, 30 hours doing administrative work and 10 hours building his practice, his practice will grow at a steady rate, and he can increase his billable work until it conflicts with the 30 required hours of administrative work he must complete. If Eric hires someone to perform his administrative work for him, he frees up 30 hours to build his practice, which then increases the number of billable hours he will be able to perform. Furthermore, because he hired someone who is an expert, it would only take her 15 hours to perform the work and would save everyone time, and give everyone more money. Efficiency is money.

It gets more complicated when you think about education. Each person has a limited amount of time to learn and develop skills and knowledge. Eric can spend his time learning legal skills in his specific field, or he can spend his time learning how to more efficiently do the administrative work. It is clear that he should spend his time learning the higher billable work, as this will provide the immediate benefit of a higher wage, but also a long term benefit of being a more desirable attorney to his clients.

The moral of this story is that your company will grow faster and be far more successful if you specialize in what you're best at, which is your comparative advantage.

Disclaimer

I've been told that the beginning of this book was rather depressing with the way I portrayed starting a business. I want to make it clear that every business I've started, whether or not it was successful, was an amazing experience that I couldn't replace with anything else. Even though there may have been stress along the way, the journey was worth every day of elevated blood pressure.

I'll give my warning now: most companies fail. If you're getting into this to make money, get out now. Statistically, entrepreneurs do not make anywhere near as much as their 9-5 counterparts. There are a few that make millions, but they're fewer than our culture leads on. The real reward comes from building something that is yours, creating relationships, developing as a person, having more flexibility, and being able to have the impact that you want to have in the company you've made. Some people get into business to make a change, some do it to have more control, some to have the flexibility, and many other reasons. As long as your reasoning isn't based on a get-rich-quick mentality, hold onto your reason and it will make you happy and successful in your own definition.

The lawyer in me felt the need to make sure you were adequately warned. Now that that's out of the way, I want to remind you that starting a business is one experience that you cannot get anywhere else, and it is an amazing one.

PART 1
READINESS

CHAPTER 1 - EMOTIONAL READINESS

Starting a business is the most taxing, stressful, time-consuming decision I've ever made that I wouldn't want to go through again, but would never trade in for anything. - Richard Bobholz

---

Starting a business involves long hours, uncertain payments and a constant stream of shattered dreams and lost hope, but it is also the most rewarding experience most entrepreneurs have ever faced professionally.

Despite all of the downsides, so many people absolutely love being an entrepreneur for many unique reasons. Just like no two companies are alike, no two entrepreneurs are alike. You must decide for yourself whether or not you are emotionally ready to start your own company. To help you with that, you should decide if you can take all of this and still be satisfied with your decision.

Tip: Knowing yourself is one of the biggest advantages as an entrepreneur. We all have strengths and weaknesses, so knowing how to take full advantage of your strengths will give you an enormous leg up in this world.

Being introspective is important. A person who is less affected by negative results (or one that thrives off of failure) is the most successful entrepreneur. Especially in the early years, letdown and loss are more common than success, but these letdowns and losses should be viewed as market research, learning experiences, and moments to make you work harder.

[ ] Step 1 -   You should answer the following questions to help you position yourself moving forward:

Why do you want to start your own business?

What things in your life are more important than your company's success?

If you've had three consecutive months where everything has gone wrong and you're losing money, which is your first reaction:
(1) close down or sell your business,
(2) hire a coach/consultant to help,
(3) revisit something that has worked well for you in the past,
(4) get motivated to work even harder,
(5) find out what is to blame for the downturn,
(6) take out a loan to reinvest, or
(7) remain unchanged in your efforts?

Why did you choose the answer to the previous question?

Would you be able to find success even if your company is consistently losing money or not performing at the level you expect?

These are all questions you must ask yourself before you start because they help you determine your emotional preparedness. There's no right answer to any of them, but be careful of any answers that measure success in dollars or place the blame on factors outside of your control. Sure, money is necessary to support our lifestyles and things outside our control can harm our companies;

however, we cannot learn when we don't acknowledge where we can improve.

Full dedication is a necessity when starting a business. Everyone thinks they'll be the exception to this rule, but you cannot start a successful company without completely dedicating to it. The level of dedication varies between companies and individuals; however, the rate of acceleration is directly proportional to the level of commitment you've made. If you leave the door open, you'll spend more time analyzing if you should walk away and less time actually building the company. You may even be hesitant about taking on long-term customers. This thought that you can always give up will ruin your company. Once you decide you're ready to start a company, burn your ships. Any opportunity to run away is an increased chance to fail.

Burning your ships is different from burning your safety net. Your retirement security is not something to risk. Put simply, you should quit trying to work a fulltime job and start a company at the same time, but don't give up anything you cannot afford to give up. Starting a company is two fulltime jobs put together, so there is no way you would be able to successfully do so while working another fulltime job. Even the most energetic person would show signs of fatigue fairly quickly.

Companies Fail

The percentages vary depending on who you ask, but you will find that a striking number of startups fail in their first years. This statistic also varies wildly based on industry. If your industry requires a lot of work and few buyers, like business-to-business software, your rate of failure is higher than ones that require either little or no capital.

For example, a consulting company or financial advising firm require very little capital input and relatively little upfront work to get started. Those types of industries require that you sell your expertise and level of service. A large percentage still fail, but the rates are lower and the reasons for failure are different. Because of the lower risk from an investment standpoint, there are also far more people who get into these industries, cutting your profit margins significantly.

Brace yourself. Instead of believing you'll fail, simply redefine success. Success should be measured in small periodic, attainable, and measurable goals. Your goals should rarely be focused entirely on revenue, profit or cash flow. Instead, measure success in new potentials, closed clients and similar numerical statistics that are wholly within your control. Even if you're bleeding money, when you measure success in these ways, you'll stay positive about your venture. Your goals should be focused on things completely under your control. Allowing others to control whether or not you're successful creates a system where your happiness and wellbeing is left up to chance.

Personal Goals

Personal goals should drive your professional goals, not the other way around. Some of these personal goals are the same things that drive you to become an entrepreneur, and others are the things you'd do no matter what.

[ ] Step 2 - To start out your journey, it is important to have goals. Take this time to write down your 1, 2, 3, 5, 10, and 20 year personal goals. To some people, these goals involve retirement, having children, buying a house, moving to Florida and other lifestyle plans that you'd like to see achieved.

Support System

The ride may be rough, but it's the fun part. When things are tough, however, you will need people there who can help build you back up. Your support system is one of the most critical items in your business. No one does this alone and success is not made in a vacuum. We need other people to fill the gaps in our psyche. When we're depressed about our failures or lack of success, we need people to remind us how far we've come or realign what success is to us. When we get lost in the details of our company, we need others to help us by reminding us what our goals are and why we are in business for ourselves.

There has been a lot of discussion recently about the unspoken psychological impact of entrepreneurship, so please, if you're ever feeling depressed or down on yourself, reach out to those in your life who will always love and support you. Despite what people may show on the surface, every entrepreneur has his or her down moments and can be a great person to talk to if you need someone.

Tip: Consider creating a group of entrepreneurs who are just getting started like you. Meet with them regularly to vent, share stories, and be able to relax. This isn't a referral group, but rather a support group for each other. This will give you extra energy and help you realize you're not alone.

To keep your support system happy, constantly remind them how important they are to you. Send them thank you cards, do random acts of kindness, bake them food, say thank you as often as you can and tell others how thankful you are to have them. Do something special for your support system as often as you can because they're your strength when you're down. Whatever you do, do not burn these bridges. As bad as things are, these people are the ones who will be there when things get worse, so keep them close. Never take out your frustration on them, and apologize when you've done them wrong. Take time out of your busy schedule to listen when they need you as their support system.

[ ] Step 3 -   Make a list of your family and friends that you can depend on for emotional support.

Significant Other Ready?

If you're married or in some form of relationship, your significant other is the most important part of your support system. Never let him or her down. He or she is far more important than your business, and I hope you never forget that. People change after major life events. Starting your own business is a major life event, and all too often it causes couples to drift apart. To avoid this, you should do the things you do for others in your support system and you should make time for them. Do not 'schedule' them in. You should make it apparent that your significant other comes first and treat him or her as such.

There are scores of books on keeping your spouse happy, but the point is that it is important to ensure that your significant other is still significant to you. The goal of your business is to make money to provide for your loved ones. Do not neglect your loved ones on the way or you will have nothing left to work for.

Kids Ready?

If you have children, you need to make sure they are ready and understand what this means for them. Your kids will have to understand your long hours, less pay and different stressors that occur in your new life. Although I am sure that you've more than considered how you have to change your work life to cater toward your kids, have you considered how to change your home life to cater toward the requirements of your new career?

Each person has different values. Some people value family, others value money. There are many different values out there, and people have their own goals and experiences that lead them to what they place value on. Especially if your value system revolves around family, you will need to constantly ensure that your children understand what you're doing and why it is important to you and to them.

If you can get your children involved in the business, they'll take some ownership in it and will understand what you do better. You should not, however, rely on your children for labor. If you treat them like employees, they'll treat you like a boss, and not a parent. Find out what they'd like to be involved in and support them in taking on that role.

Understand What You're Getting Into

In order to ensure that you do not become disappointed with your decision to start your own business, you should pay close attention to this part. We're going to examine what it actually means to start your own business. We will look at the pros and cons as well as the physical and emotional effects it has on you.

Long Hours

Typically, your hours will be much longer than in a 9-to-5 career. It is not unheard of to work a one hundred hour week every now and then. Sixty to eighty hours of work is common. Time management is something we will examine later in this book. With proper time management, you can get done in twenty hours what would take others one hundred. Your ability to become a better time manager greatly depends on your industry and you personally, but everyone can afford to become more efficient.

Despite the long hours, you can choose them. Never forget that you can take time off for the important things in life. I know many entrepreneur parents who work well into the night after their kids go to bed because they want to spend as much time with their children as possible. This is an option. You just have to keep in mind what is important to you.

Unusual Hours

Long hours usually come with unusual hours. It is not uncommon to work late nights planning for your company, or weekends when your customers need you to. Fortunately, you're able to set your own hours and can therefore schedule your work around important family events. As everyone who has started a business knows, you will end up working even when you're not at work. Many entrepreneurs find themselves working late into the night or waking up earlier to work on your company or catch up on work. Especially in project-based companies, entrepreneurs find themselves working incredibly long hours, as they get caught up in their work. Business owners get caught up in the thing they are passionate about and wind up working hours well beyond those a typical 9-5 works.

If you expect the constant nine-to-five job, it's still possible, and if this is your measure of success, you can easily obtain it. For other entrepreneurs, the measure of success comes after significantly more than 40-hour work weeks, and there will be moments where you'll be working late into the night or scribbling on napkins at social functions.

Life and Work Blend

A typical entrepreneur will struggle nearly every week with distinguishing between personal life and business life. This seemingly never goes away. It will either require a vast amount of discipline or a large amount of time scheduling to ensure that your two worlds do not collide. The smarter business owner finds ways to combine these two worlds. Taking your friends and family to more family-centered or social networking events is one of the many great ways to combine these two worlds. Wine tastings, fancy dinners and activity-based events are usually more social and can be great experiences for your family. These, however, do not replace dedicated family time.

On the flip side, you should be friendly with your customers, but you are not friends. Your customers will appreciate the fact that you keep things professional. Otherwise, your customers will expect free services or reduced price "friend rates" because they're your friend. Friends also usually value the product or service they receive from a friend less than that of a non-familiar acquaintance. The telltale sign of losing your customers to your own friendliness is when they frequently get second opinions or they say the phrase, "do you think I should talk to a _____?" or a "real _____."

For example: You're a business consultant and you recommend a certain action for the direction of your client's business. If she asks whether or not she should seek the advice of a business consultant or a real business consultant, you're in the "friend zone." You may be laughing, but this actually happens quite often to many different consultant or professional businesses. For products, you'll start receiving requests to sell items at cost or donate items to support a cause or to "promote your business."

The moral of the story is that you should not use your customers to replace your social life. The way you interact with your friends is inappropriate for interactions with your customers, and the way you interact with your customers is an inappropriate way to treat your friends and family.

Some entrepreneurs believe that it is okay to work seven days a week, sixteen hours a day. For most people, this can be very damaging. It isn't just about a person's health. Constant work also yields diminishing returns. Everyone needs a break, but it is difficult to realize just how burned out you may have become.

There was an owner that worked for a year straight before finally taking a day off. He took a week vacation and when he came back, he managed to get through more items on his checklist in one day than he did in a week before his vacation. He was burned out, but because he was burned out, he couldn't possibly realize just how exhausted he was. The week allowed him to recharge his batteries and his business started taking off again.

Sometimes, all we need is to step away from the problem for a while and then come back and take control again. Consider vacation time as an investment. As you would gladly spend a week implementing new software that made you 50% more efficient, you should also gladly drop everything and hit the beach for a week so that you can return refreshed and more efficient.

Tip: Create a work-free space. This space will help you relax and clear your mind. Never do work in that space and you will be able to rejuvenate faster and be far more efficient.

Creative juices also recharge with changed circumstances. Visiting the same problem over and over again without giving yourself a chance to look at it from another angle or gain inspiration from other places is not an effective use of your time. Sometimes, all it takes is a walk, a shower, or something relaxing to get the creativity flowing again. Whatever works for you, find it and utilize it when necessary. It's not procrastination if the purpose of you putting it off is to do a better job. A break allows you to become more efficient later, so take advantage of breaks and let yourself off the hook for not working for a little while.

Tip: As with creating a work-free space, you should create a work-only space. This will help keep you focused and can also help for tax purposes when deducting a portion of your house exclusively used for business.

Do Your Family/Friends Understand?

It's not about the money. Contrary to what the media portray, starting your own company isn't about the money. Your family and friends, however, will likely believe that you're in business for yourself because you want to make it rich. If you're not rich after six months, they're going to wonder what you've done wrong. If your idea is based around a product, they'll likely believe in that product because you made it, but they won't understand why you haven't made millions. Those outside the process cannot understand how things work. It's important for you to explain to them how it works and why you're doing what you do. By simply educating your family and friends on why you chose this path, you'll have a much stronger support system.

When you explain to your family and friends why you're in business for yourself, you'll let them into the circle, showing them just how hard it is for you to run this company, where you need them to help you out and why this is so important to you that you'd give up any other career path. If you want to keep them happy, which you do, you will have to let them in early enough that they understand why you're in the career you are in.

[ ] Step 4 -   At this point, before you get too deeply involved in the startup process, it is a good idea to write letters to your family, children (if any), and friends. These are the people who will be your support system going forward, so use this opportunity to thank them in advance, tell them why they're your support system, explain to them what they should expect and tell them what you'll need from them going forward. The better you know yourself, the better these letters can be because you know how you'll become when you're stressed or feeling overwhelmed. A sample letter can be found in Appendix V.

Values

Before delving into the business side of things, we still need to figure out what's important to you. If you start, as we are, with your values, it is actually very easy to make business decisions in the future.

Your values are a very important starting point for planning your business. Everything you do as part of your business will go toward your values. Anything done that goes against your defined values would be a source of friction and would slow your potential growth and drain you of energy. Therefore, anything that goes against your values hurts your company.

This is your company so it should reflect the things you hold dearest. Some examples of values people hold include freedom, love, kindness, honesty, simplicity and quality work. These examples should not be a guide for your own values because each person is different. Your goals will generally reflect what's important to you. For example, if one of your goals was to spend more time with your children, family is a very important value to you.

If you choose values that do not actually fit your personality, you will struggle to uphold the values you've set, so pick things you know you hold and not things that you aspire to hold.

Stick with values you're already comfortable with. If they're natural to uphold, it won't take you any energy or thought later on.

The decisions will be more natural.

▌[ ] Step 5 -   Write down a list of all of your personal values.

Measure of Success

Our capitalist society teaches us to measure success in monetary terms; however, I'm telling you to fight that urge.

Success can be defined in countless ways. Money is arguably the worst way to measure success. We work to get money. Money allows us to make our standard of living better. There are, however, many things that also allow us to have a higher standard of living. These other things are where you measure success.

From a goal-setting perspective, the amount of money you have is arbitrary. You give up thousands of hours a year working in exchange for money at a job, but if you're self-employed, you give up even more hours to have the hopes of getting paid. Your payment is subject to an incredible number of variables including the desires of your customers, the economy, bills you never saw coming and more. You should never leave your happiness in the hands of so many variables. The uncertainty alone will create unnecessary stress that will lessen your productivity and, therefore, lower your success. It's a vicious cycle, so you shouldn't measure your success in such variable terms.

Success can, and should, be more under your control. You can measure it through specific quantifiable goals. For example, you can set a goal to make it to ten networking events or to meet with sixty new contacts in a month. With goals like these, you are the only one who can determine whether or not you achieve your goal, meaning that your failure or success is less uncertain, and therefore, less stressful. Furthermore, you will have to accept the entire blame for failing to meet these goals, leaving you more accountable to yourself.

Achieving success and reaching your goals gives you fuel to reach the next goal whereas failure, especially repeated failures, will add stress to your life and make it harder to complete the work you need to get done.

You wear stress like a bad perfume. The more of it you have, the less likely people will want to do business with you. The more devoid of stress you are, the more people will want to be around you. It's unfortunate, but those who are the most desperate also have the hardest time making sales.

> [ ] Step 6 -   Create your own definition of success. This should be based on the reasons you want to be self-employed. For example, success to you could be being able build a respectable brand in the community and being recognized for doing great work, if you felt unrecognized and underutilized working for someone else. Do not base success on whether or not your company earns you money.

Uncertain Outcomes

The best laid plans...

Even the best plans can go astray, and sometimes this means that you will suffer hardship, no matter how carefully you planned. Even if you do absolutely everything right, things can turn out quite unlike how you expected because that's the nature of owning a small business. You rely on so many outside forces in your business that your day-to-day operations are largely out of your control. Like a stream of water, the best you can do is try to reroute it a little bit at a time.

By expecting a specific outcome and receiving another, you set yourself up to become frustrated with your business. It's best to plan for favorable outcomes, but it is foolish to think things will always turn out the way you planned.

You should expect things to go slightly awry. Through this expectation, you will gain more satisfaction and higher morale when things go better than you planned. This will help build you up so that you will have less stress and higher self-esteem thereby creating far more success personally and in your career.

Tip: Look for ways you can fail intentionally as learning experiences. If there's nothing on the line, it may benefit you to see what happens if you fail.

Emotional readiness is one part of the puzzle. The emotional side concerns your psychological wellbeing opposed to your financial wellbeing. Failure to prepare for this could result in hatred of your once-loved career choice. You must always love what you do because your extrinsic reward (cash) is going to be small by comparison to an established career at a larger company. The intrinsic reward is the only thing you can rely on for continued internal emotional support; therefore, you must ensure you always understand and believe in what you're doing.

Getting Help When Needed

Unfortunately, there is an epidemic among entrepreneurs. If you ever feel overwhelmed, overly stressed, or you can't see any options in front of you, I sincerely hope you take my advice to get professional help. Business owners like you and I face much higher chances of suffering from depression and anxiety than the general population, and it's very hard for us to admit when there is something wrong.

I completely understand why it is hard for us to admit when there's something wrong. Anytime we don't look successful to our potential customers, we're less likely to secure that sale.

I've seen too many of my friends and colleagues slip into depression, or worse, and it is something we can all help prevent. If you're feeling helpless, seek help. If you think one of your colleagues may be depressed or suffering from uncontrollable anxiety, help that person realize it is okay to get help.

Hopefully it will help you to know that I've been there. I've received counseling for depression, and that counseling was the best choice I've made. Remember, depression and anxiety are very common among entrepreneurs, so you are not alone. Being strong is getting help so you can get back to building your company.

[ ] Step 7 - Make a promise to yourself to get help should you need it.

CHAPTER 2 - FINANCIAL READINESS

Financial readiness, like emotional readiness, is very important. Almost no new companies make any significant money for at least six months. In fact, many of them do not make any money for three to five years, depending on the industry and business model. For example, a new product may take three years to make it to market after extensive testing. Service industries will start generating cash quicker, but the cash flow is typically slow in the beginning.

Income Coverage

Before you start your business, you should prepare a budget for everything you will need money for in the upcoming three to five years. Relying on the assumption that you know you'll make money is a huge mistake. You should calculate rent, utilities, food, vacations, Christmas presents, etc. and formulate a month-by-month spreadsheet. Working with a financial advisor can really help this process. Typically, full service financial advisors do not charge for this service as part of a larger representation.

[ ] Step 8 -   List all personal expenses. Utilities, car, gifts, mortgage, food, etc. Overestimate the expenses when you're unsure.

[ ] Step 9 -   List all sources of personal income.

Either you'll need all the cash up front in savings or you'll need some form of reliable cash flow to fund your way through. Keep in mind that investors do not pay your salary. If you find one that does, be prepared for a lot of strings attached. Their money can curb the cost of the business itself, but you're still going to need money every month to survive.

> [ ] Step 10 - Make a month-by-month individual budget of your first 3 years, excluding any income from your business at this time. A sample budget can be found on the website at www.checkmarkstartup.com/resources

If you have negative cash flow at this point, that is fine. This negative cash flow is called a budget deficit. In this particular sense, you can have a budget deficit, as long as you have enough in savings to cover your first 6 months to 3 years. You have to make sure you're comfortable covering this amount, or you should find things to cut in your budget or other sources of income. Keep in mind we haven't even looked at business expenses yet.

If you have positive cash flow at this point, that's great. That will make getting into business easier because you won't have to worry as much about covering your personal expenses.

For many people, they have a spouse or family that supports them. For others, they've saved enough money in their savings to make this work. No matter where the money comes from, you're going to have to be the one who makes the budgets and is very careful with the money.

Certificates of Deposit are great tools for ensuring you do not use up all of your funds at once. Since you can set them up in six month intervals, you can arrange to have the money become available every six months, so the worst you can do is waste six months' worth of savings. It is recommended to use tools like CDs if you're not incredibly responsible with your money. It has to last, so you should do whatever it takes to do so.

Bootstrapping

Companies cost money. If you are not receiving any money from outside the company and your personal finances, you are bootstrapping the company. This simply means you are paying for everything yourself and have no investment funds from which to pull cash from.

Bootstrapping is a very noble way to run a company and gives you a far greater sense of satisfaction once it has become successful; however, it is hard. Since it is all your money, every dollar you spend on the company is a dollar you would not have to spend on things like gifts for your loved ones or vacations for yourself. In more dire circumstances, you may even have to choose between food and your company. Hopefully, you will not reach that point, but you may find yourself going out less because you see the value of your money in different terms.

[ ] Step 11 - Write down all the estimated costs of running your business each month.

[ ] Step 12 - Using your personal budget, put these estimated business costs in as additional expenses to see what revenue you absolutely must generate to meet your total expenses.

Although we still haven't included any business revenue, you have an idea of how much you need to invest of your own money, loans, or investments to make your company succeed. If you still have a budget surplus, you're in a great position. If you have a deficit, either cut costs or find ways to cover the expenses.

Loans

Loans are one way to finance your company. Small business loans are often cited as great ideas for small businesses; however, there are plenty of people who would disagree with that notion entirely.

Small business loans typically require a cosigner because the company is too young to have any credit. This can be a very bad idea! When a bank requires you to cosign on a loan, they're saying they don't trust the company to pay back the loan. Therefore, they're putting that risk on you personally. If the company goes under, the bank will look to your savings, your home, your car, and everything else they can get to cover the cost of the loan.

This means that you're increasing the liability on yourself. This personal liability should be avoided. Typically, when you form an LLC or corporation, the maximum you can lose is the value of the company. We will discuss this limited liability later on in this book; however, you should know that any time you need to sign personally for the company, you're increasing the risk that you carry yourself. It is generally not worth cosigning on anything that increases the risk to you personally.

If your company needs loans, and it cannot get the money on its own credit, you should consider looking for investors, looking for alternate forms of funding, or closing down the company. If your company is showing signs of failure, and that's why you need the money, you should consider closing the company before taking out a small business loan that you have to cosign.

Tip: Some loans are less risky to you personally, like loans for capital equipment or to purchase an existing business because you're buying something with resale value. Loans for marketing or wages, don't come with the same collateral.

If you need money because your cash flow cannot support the business growth, speak with an accountant, CPA, or lawyer who works in this area to find out if a small business loan is worth the cost. Investors are typically better, but an accountant, CPA, or lawyer would be able to examine and see if the interest rate on the loan is worth it in your particular situation while always keeping in mind the added personal risk.

Loans require that you pay them back, and in the beginning, there's almost always personal liability for those loans. Furthermore, in the beginning of most companies, the return on investment (ROI) is very low, typically fractions of a percent. You should only consider loans if your ROI is higher than the interest rate on the loan. This is something your accountant, CPA or financial planner should explain to you.

Loans take away from cash flow, and cash flow is king. Anytime you're sacrificing cash flow, you're stunting the growth of your company. Therefore, you should do a careful analysis to ensure you have the cash flow to support the loan and other programs that require cash flow, like wages and inventory. Also, be mindful of other things you'd want to use cash flow for, such as marketing, capital investments, and expansion.

Certain industries, such as medical, almost always require a loan to start, but that's to purchase medical equipment. Banks rarely have to go after a doctor personally compared to other types of businesses.

The moral of this section is be very cautious around loans, especially if you have to cosign them.

Family and Friends

A lot of companies are supported by family and friends. There are a lot of people in the startup community that call this 'dumb' money implying that the friends or family are not all that savvy. However, this is not dumb money so much as it is loving money. Many times the money is invested with more information than any professional investor.

Tip: Any time you take money from friends or family, make sure you undersell yourself. As long as they understand the great risk you're taking, they'll be less upset should things go wrong.

Most families with any significant amount of money have that money because they refused to part ways with it without a good reason. Furthermore, they have far greater understanding of who they are investing in since they've known this person longer than any investor could have.

However you classify the money, it is dumb to let it go to waste. Taking money from your friends and families has a far greater chance of becoming a personal disaster rather than just a business transaction. If your company fails and you were supported by an investor, the investor is upset, but that's all; however, if your family or friends supported you and you lost their money, you will hear about it again and again.

Furthermore, you need your family and friends as a vital part of your support structure. If you fail when they invested in your company, they may not be there when you need them to be. Taking money from friends and family turns them from your emotional support system into your financial support system, and these two roles are very different. Always ensure your emotional support system is well stocked. If you only have a few people in that role, don't take their money.

Investors

Investors are a great way to fund your company, but once again, this route shouldn't be done without appropriate consideration. It is true that well-funded companies have a far greater chance of success; however, you need to ensure that you need the money and that you'd use it for company-building purposes. Many successful companies only need the owner's time and no capital investment. If that's the case, there's no reason to take on investors.

Investors take equity (percentage ownership in your company), and they invest to make a profit. The valuation of the company by an investor will be far lower than your own valuation. They value your company based on projected cash flow and assets. You value your company on projected cash flow, assets and potential. The investor does not care about the potential like you do; therefore, you will always see their valuation lower than yours.

Typically, an investor's valuation of the projected cash flow will also be lower than yours because their valuation is more linear than yours is. Put another way, you will envision more acceleration in the growth of your company than an investor will. If you value your company at a million dollars and want one hundred thousand dollars, you should expect to give up ten percent of your company; however, if they value your company at two hundred thousand dollars, you will have to give up fifty percent of your company in order to receive the same investment.

Seeking investors take time that you could otherwise spend building the company. It takes many months to prepare proposals, meet with investors, pitch to investors, plan out the paperwork, restructure your company, and do all the things involved in seeking out investments. Throughout this process, you'll likely be learning new things as well. Any time spent seeking an investment is time you're not spending building your business.

Some people believe that investors are the only way to build a high-impact company, and that's the major goal they work for until they achieve it; however, the investor is just one route toward funding, and it's a route that takes up a lot of time. Once you actually get an investor, you will likely have to provide reports and have meetings to ensure the company is growing. There is value in these things, but they still take time that you could be using on higher value items.

Tip: Talk to people you've met who have investors and those who don't. Find out the benefits and costs from their perspectives.

Your time is the only commodity that you cannot get more of. Once it is gone, it is gone. In any startup, it is also the trading commodity. You typically do not have the money, capital goods or technology, so what you offer is your time and your skills.

Investors come with strings. How many owners do you want weighing in on every decision? Rarely do you find an investor that loves the company exactly how it is. Because of this, they will ask for you to make some changes in order to receive their investment. Some changes might be minor, like having to document standard procedures, and others may be major, like changes in the management of the company itself.

Giving up equity to an investor may yield significant changes in the company, but it tends to bring more success. A common phrase in the entrepreneurial world is "I'd rather own 1% of something than 100% of nothing," meaning that if your company fails, like most do, you will have nothing, so it is wiser to give up as much company as is necessary to make sure it succeeds. Make sure that if you choose to use investors, you use the money they provide to build the business and not on extraneous secondary expenditures. Carefully weigh the cost of getting an investor, taking into account the time, control and value you give up to gain an investor.

Every type of financial setup for your company comes with its pros and cons. Here's a schedule of each of the methods mentioned above:

	Bootstrapping	Own Cash Investment	Family / Friends	Loans	Investors
Acceleration	Low	Mid	Mid	Low	High
Equity Surrender	None	None	None/Low	None	High
Personal Liability	Mid	High	Mid	High	Low
Time Surrender	None	None	Low/Mid	Mid	High
Strings	None	None	None/Low	Low	High
Other Cost	None	Savings	Emotional	None	None

[ ] Step 13 - Using the above information, decide how you plan on financing your company, if it is determined that you need additional money to cover the first few years.

CHAPTER 3 - COMPANY VALUES AND MISSION STATEMENT

Your company values are those that you've picked from your personal values that you want your company to reflect. Hopefully your personal values and the values you want your company to have will mesh up nicely. There is no magic rule to how many values you've decided for your company. The fewer you have, the more specific you will be able to target each value, so having too many will dilute your brand. Conversely, having too few might stymie your ability to create brand awareness. For our process, pick ten values for your company.

[ ] Step 14 - Taking your personal values list, circle the values you want your company to have.

Mesh With Personal Values

Once you've got the list of your personal values and your company values, put them side-by-side and choose the ones you want to focus on as a company and a brand. Your company should still have the longer list of values for reference, but there should be no more than three that you're going to focus on. Because you don't want to dilute your branding efforts, you'll want to be fairly specific in your choices.

You should also make sure there is significant overlap between your personal values and your company values in the choices you will focus on. If they are completely distinct, your personal efforts will not help your company brand and when you're working on your company brand, you will exhaust yourself. The values you already have personally come naturally to you and working on those does not create the friction that wears you down.

Your list of chosen values will be referenced in many decisions your company makes down the road, especially when it comes to marketing. You shouldn't do any marketing without addressing this list. If you've chosen well, the decisions will not take any additional time or effort on your part.

> [ ] Step 15 - Using your company value list from the previous step, choose 3-5 values that will make up your company's brand. These will be the ones you focus on in every decision.

Before you can write your mission statement, you really need to do some public relations work to determine how you want the public to perceive your company.

A mission statement is a short statement describing the company's values and purpose that will remain unchanged, for the most part, over the passage of time. After your company's values, this will be the most static part of your company.

> [ ] Step 16 - Write a one-sentence reason why each of your values is necessary or appreciated by those who would want your product or service.

The mission statement itself is the slogan or motto of your company that drives the decision-making process. It should include what the company does, how it does it, and some company values.

> [ ] Step 17 - Write down a complete list of the products or services your company provides.

> [ ] Step 18 - Write down the problem your company solves.

Typically, a mission statement is between one sentence and one paragraph long, but there really are no rules as long as it is something you can create, memorize and stick to.

[ ] Step 19 - Using your list of products or services, the problem your company solves and your company values from before, create a mission statement for your company. If you don't have a name yet, it is fine to leave the name blank or just not include a name.

Sample Mission Statement: _____ solves <problem> by providing <adjective> <service> to <demographic> while focusing on <value 1>, <value 2>, and <value 3>

[ ] Step 20 - Read your mission statement to yourself 10 times aloud to make sure it is something you could roll off your tongue.

CHAPTER 4 - GOALS

The goal is an item missing from most business plans. Especially with the small business, it is incredibly important. It's the most important part from a personal standpoint. You need to have a goal in order to achieve any amount of success. Whether or not you achieve your goal, you're working toward something. In this case, you should make it a measurable, specific goal that is achievable.

Some of the more common goals of small businesses are some variation of the following:

- Build a product and sell it in 3-5 years
- Create a company that will provide income and jobs for my children
- Build a company that will provide me income in retirement
- Earn enough money that I don't have to work for someone else

There are, of course, countless other goals that people have, but they always revolve around some intrinsic value like independence, security or comfort. In your case, this goal should relate very closely to your personal goals and be reflective of your chosen business values.

▌[ ] Step 21 - Create your goal.

SMART Goals

The goals above, although they would be great outcomes, would be poor goals to have. Better goals are SMART. SMART stands for specific, measurable, attainable, relevant and time-bound.

A specific goal is one that contains specific details. You're looking for numbers and something where you can see a determinate end. They cannot be lofty and floating around. A goal such as "make a lot of money" is not specific. A better example would be "to make one hundred thousand in the first year in revenue"; however, we're going to avoid money-related goals. Picking goals that you cannot control have a higher tendency to lead to dissatisfaction and can therefore lower your determination and excitement toward your career.

A measurable goal needs numbers or a way to know when the goal is met or what percent of the goal is met. Although your goals are tied to intrinsic values (which are immeasurable), you still need some level of measurability. The goal from above had one hundred thousand in the first year. This is a measurable goal because you could easily calculate what percent you had achieved at any given date.

Attainable goals are important because they determine whether or not you will believe in your own goals. If you set a goal to sell your company for thirty-two billion dollars in three years, it is likely that is not an attainable goal for almost every business.

Relevant goals are ones that pertain to your ultimate goal and your business model. If you run a software company, you should not have goals that do not relate to your software company or your ultimate goal under the business plan.

Time-bound goals are ones that have a deadline. You must set yourself a deadline or you will likely not work toward the goal. Most people are very good at procrastinating. A project will create more 'work' as long as that project is not yet at its deadline. Some things can be done in one month that are given three to do and yet, they still take three months because they do not have a deadline fast approaching. As such, goals that do not have an approaching deadline will linger forever. They will only be accomplished accidentally.

▌[ ] Step 22 - Turn your goal into a SMART goal.

Milestones

Creating milestones that you want to reach with specific dates in mind is a necessary step in the goal-setting process. The following is a goal that is expanded and better than those above:

Goal: To design our product, formulate a team and engage with 1,100 customers in the following manner:

1. Stage 1 of product (design and wireframe) by 1/10/17
2. Interview 10 developers by 1/15/17
3. Second round interview 3 developers by 1/25/17
4. Meet 100 people networking by 2/10/17
5. Select developer by 2/10/17
6. Stage 2 of product (back end development and JSON structure) by 4/1/17
7. Meet 300 people networking by 4/10/17
8. And so on...

As you can see in this goal, there are specific milestones with dates needed to be met. This specificity and end date provides you with motivation to accomplish them.

[ ] Step 23 - Break your SMART goal into specific sub goals with milestones, creating a roadmap from where you are today to where you want to be. The first steps are already completed for you, as this book helps set up your company for success.

Writing down your goal puts it in the forefront of your mind, where it should be. If you want to achieve your goal, it should be a deciding factor in every decision you make. If the decision would lead you away from your ultimate goal, it's the wrong decision. As such, your goal should be in line with your values. If you value spending time with your family, your goals should not be about anything that doesn't give you the time to spend with your family.

As your values change, so can your goal, but that's the beauty of a business plan. It can change as often as you'd like.

In order to achieve your larger goal, you will want to create many sub-goals. These should be SMART goals as well. Properly set up sub-goals will look like a step-by-step plan to your ultimate goal. This will be your game plan.

PART 2
THE BUSINESS PLAN

CHAPTER 5 - PRODUCTS AND SERVICE

The business plan is your guidebook. This is the element of your business that you should put the most amount of thought into early on, but be aware that this will change frequently as you progress through your journey.

A well written business plan will save you countless hours in the future and help you accelerate in the correct direction. A cliché in wood working is "measure twice, cut once," and that phrase really applies here. The work you put in saves you exponential work down the road.

The business plan is an outline of what you intend to do and how you intend to do it. It breaks down how your company is to be run, from marketing and finance to production and operations.

To help you, we've created the outline for your business plan. You can find it on the website or in Appendix I.

You should expect this process to take you several days. If you wrote your business plan in an hour, it isn't finished. Even for the smallest businesses, this planning portion should take you several days and be incredibly well thought out. By taking the time now, you accelerate your business dramatically and even avoid countless pitfalls you would have otherwise landed into.

An ounce of prevention is worth a pound of cure. -
Benjamin Franklin.

If your business is separated into departments, each department should have its own micro business plan. The department would have its own values based on the values of the company as well as its own goals and processes. Most successful companies should start with just one department and then branch out. There are, sometimes, reasons to have multiple departments in a company that is just starting. As long as the departments are kept straight, and managed separately, they can still succeed very well.

You've already written your goals and mission statement. Those go into the business plan as well.

Getting Help

There are countless resources out there to help you with your business plan. If you already have a small business attorney, business coach, CPA or mentor, he or she should be able to give you the resources you need to make this work for you, and they will give you those resources that they have found work best and work with the way they work with your business. I'd highly recommend using the resources your trusted advisor gives you because it will make incorporating the business plan with other areas of the process much simpler.

If you don't have these resources already in place, you can do some research. You may want to start at sba.gov for their amazing list of resources for small business owners, including help making a business plan. You can also search for examples off which you would like to base your company or look to MBA or financial planning colleges in your local universities. Some universities even have clinics that will help you create a business plan in person.

And if you need more places to turn for help, there are also local businesses called incubators that help jumpstart your business. Even if you're not in the incubator, these places frequently put on programs that help the general public, like seminars on business plan writing.

Description of Product/Services

Before you can sell a product or service, you will need to know exactly what it is you are selling. This analysis should be made at the highest level and the most micro of levels. At the highest level, an insurance salesman sells peace of mind and financial security. At the micro level, he would describe each and every product in the insurance portfolio in the finest of details. If he cannot do this, he's unable to sell his product to the best of his ability and will frequently lose clients to insurance salespeople who are able to adequately describe their products.

[ ] Step 24 -   Using the list of products or services, add the product or service to the template business plan that is included. An electronic copy can be found at www.checkmarkstartup.com.

[ ] Step 25 -   For each product or service you included in the template, add a detailed description of what is included in that product or service. The description should include what your customer gets, what values are fulfilled, what new needs result and any other opportunity cost or benefit.

The value your customer receives is very different from the value you place on the product or service. Consumers only ever buy a product or service when the perceived value exceeds the price they pay for it.

[ ] Step 26 -   For each product or service, list the benefits the consumer receives.

Consumers also only buy things that fulfill intrinsic needs. These intrinsic needs are the only things that we use to make decisions, but through chaining, we've associated certain other things with our fulfillment of intrinsic needs.

These needs include: safety, social, food, water, sex, self-actualization, self-esteem, air, shelter, and a few others along these lines.

[ ] Step 27 - For each product or service, list the intrinsic needs that are fulfilled, or the chain that leads to an intrinsic need. For example, virtual assistants free up time, which increases productivity which increases revenue which provides peace of mind and security. If you cannot identify the intrinsic need your product or service fulfills, or a route to an intrinsic need, you should eliminate that product or service.

Example: Bananas fulfill hunger.

As said before, consumers weigh benefit versus cost. The cost is anything they have to give up. This includes money, time, sacrifice of any other intrinsic needs, and anything else the consumer has to part with.

[ ] Step 28 - For each product or service, list the cost, excluding the money you charge.

CHAPTER 6 - MARKETING

Marketing Plan

As we discussed earlier, companies have four components: Production, Expansion, Protection, and Administration. Your marketing plan is the expansion. Without some level of marketing, your company will remain at $0 in value.

Having a plan in place makes it more manageable, more focused and more efficient. Without a plan, most business owners end up spending money on marketing in ways that do not have the desired effect on their public relations or have a lower return on the investment than other ideas that would have been selected had a marketing plan been made.

When speaking with marketing professionals, public relations specialists and outsourced chief marketing officers, it has become apparent that one of the largest marketing blunders that small businesses do is marketing through unconnected plans (the shotgun approach). The problem with this approach is that some marketing efforts can conflict with others, and becomes too much overlap. The result is a less efficient strategy through competition with yourself.

Fortunately, as we move into this portion of the business plan, you have already done a lot of the work.

[ ] Step 29 - If you're not using our provided template in Appendix I, create a document with headings for Market Analysis, Demographics, Competitors, Needs Fulfillment, Detailed Marketing Plan, and Pricing.

Market Analysis

The first step in any marketing plan is an analysis of the market. This includes an analysis of the demographic you intend to reach as well as the other people in the market already reaching that demographic, your competitors. Beyond that, you want to analyze what both a complimentary good and a supplemental good are so that you know what to partner with and what you're competing with that isn't a direct competitor.

Demographic

The next step in your market plan is analyzing who is your demographic. The better analysis you do here, the more efficient your marketing can be later, saving you time and money.

Business or Individual

Start with a very general perspective. Primarily, your demographics are broken down into Business to Business (B2B) or Business to Consumer (B2C). B2B means you're selling your product or service to businesses and B2C means your customers are individuals.

There's some overlap and other areas, like government, but we're sticking with the two primary areas. You can still do these others steps if you're not B2B or B2C.

[ ] Step 30 - Under the Demographic section, write whether you are selling to businesses or individuals.

This step clarifies things. From there, you want to break down your demographic into as many identifiable characteristics as possible. Are you targeting a specific industry? Is your audience full of women or men? What income level would purchase your service?

With each question, you paint a clearer picture of who you are targeting. Using this information, you will want to ensure that you are marketing to these individuals and not wasting your marketing time and money in areas that have less of an impact on your demographic.

Age

If the customer base is composed of individuals opposed to businesses, you want to look to your customers' age range first. Different age groups look in different places for their products and services. Identifying your optimal age group will help you identify what sources of marketing will yield the highest impact.

Race and Culture

As is the same with age, different races and cultures will also look to different sources to find their products and services. Keep in mind, this has more to do with culture than it does race.

Because of their different cultures, there are also different hierarchies of needs and wants, cultural stigmas, mannerisms, trusted icons, and other differences. Be cognizant of the differences, but do not make them the highlight of your marketing efforts. It is easy, especially if you are not a part of that culture, to insult a person or group of people because you made generalizations.

Be aware of statistical information, like where people find their news and entertainment. Do not use these generalized pieces of information to assume any one person or group of people fits into that statistical mold.

Industry

For businesses, industry really matters. For example, certain industries, like medicine, have their own trade magazines, conferences and social circles. If you're trying to reach the medical field, you're going to want to direct your efforts into those specific areas instead of reaching out to broader markets.

Gender

It should be no surprise that statistically, men and women look in different areas for their products and services. This is true due to cultural norms over biological differences, but the facts remain the same. When marketing, taking gender into account will make your marketing efforts far more effective than broad targeting.

For example, if 98% of your buyers are women, you'd want to market your efforts toward women instead of the broad spectrum marketing you would use without this research.

Specifics

If there's anything specific about your demographic that can be measured and quantified, you should narrow down your demographic in these ways as well. The more specific your criteria, the better results you will get because you'll have a much higher conversion ratio.

You want to avoid marketing to people that you know have a low probability of converting into paying customers. By creating an even more specific target demographic, you increase your chance of successful conversion. This saves you money and time.

[ ] Step 31 - List as many demographic traits as you can of your customer in the Demographic Section of your Marketing Plan.

Client Wealth

Another thing you must consider is how much money your clients have. This will largely determine what you can charge, where you seek out your clients and the highest quality you can profitably offer.

You can only charge what your customers can afford. If your goal is to offer a product that inner-city youth can afford, you had better not be charging thousands of dollars for your product. On the other hand, if you're marketing to successful businessmen and women, you have more money to work with. That said, you generally cannot just increase the price arbitrarily. You will need to raise the value as you raise the price, either through branding or quality.

Different income levels seek out information in different ways. With the advent of the internet, more people are seeking information online. Creating the most expensive website may not have the desired results if your website makes your product above or below the quality that your ideal customer expects.

Generally, the higher the quality of product, the higher its price will be. This is true because you will either have to spend more time or more money to generate the higher quality product. Of course, you should still strive to create the highest quality possible within your price range, but if you increase the quality too much and market to a demographic that cannot afford it, you will see an alarmingly low conversion rate and your company will fail.

[ ] Step 32 - Write down whether your demographic is wealthy, poor, middle class, or any other descriptors regarding income and wealth that describes your demographic.

How Much Can They Pay?

Costs come in all shapes and sizes. To some demographics, time is worth more than money. To others, the money is worth more than the time. Your job is to determine what your customers can pay. If they can pay with their time, then structure the business in a way that utilizes their time. Make them do some of the work. For example, if you run a bookkeeping service and your clients are not affluent, give them most of the work to do and come in to clean things up later. If they are affluent, they won't want to spend the time and would rather you handle every detail.

Sometimes, your customers can pay in trade, but not in money or time. If this interests you, you can always structure your business to handle this as well.

This isn't to say that you cannot reach your clients by reaching out to those areas that aren't in your demographic. Rather, this is to say that you'd be wasteful to do so.

Tip: Initially, pick the best demographic and go after them. It seems counter-intuitive but the more specific you are, the more customers you'll get. That doesn't mean you actively exclude other demographics; it means that you just market to one.

Because free market economies destroy inefficient companies., you do not want to waste your time and money in areas that are less efficient when a simple analysis brings clearer options.

[ ] Step 33 - Using the cost for each product and service you
wrote before, compare these costs with what your
customers can pay to make sure that it is something your
customers would be willing to pay; i.e. if your customers
are impoverished, you shouldn't have a costly product.

Competitors

Once you've analyzed your customers, you will want to analyze
your competitors. "Keep your friends close and your enemies
closer." Your competitors are a wonderful source of knowledge.
From their example, you can see what works and what does not. Do
not, however, assume that because your competitors have been
doing something for many years that it is the most efficient way to
do something. It may be that it is just too hard to change or they have
a stubborn corporate culture.

For your competitors, you want to determine as much as you can
about them and create miniature business guides for them. If your
industry is overly saturated, make estimations about your
competitors, like how many are there, what you have noticed that
works, what you have noticed that doesn't work, where could
improvement be made, etc?

Your competitor analysis is also useful when you analyze the size
of the market to ensure that you fit.

[ ] Step 34 - Make a list of the top 5-10 competitors within
your geographic scope, including any information
pertaining to costs, pricing, their geographic reach, their
customers, and their marketing efforts.

What Makes You Unique

When analyzing the market, you need something that sets you
apart. What makes you unique? If you're a CPA and the same as
every other CPA out there, why would anyone use you opposed to
the guy in the office next door? Most people have some reason why
they go into business for themselves opposed to working for the guy
next door. This is probably also the reason you're unique.

Do you have a piece of technology that makes your process more
streamlined? Are you more trustworthy? Do you believe that you're

friendlier and more likeable to your clients? Whatever the reason, you need to analyze what makes you unique. The more quantifiable, the better.

> [ ] Step 35 - Write down what makes you unique compared to all your competitors.

This uniqueness factor is something you will want to exploit in your marketing. It must also be a value to your company and you because it answers the question "why you opposed to the other guy?" A friend of mine asked if it would be a good idea for him to advertise his small business legal services in Polish publications because he's fluent in Polish. The answer is 'yes' because he's now set himself apart in the Polish business community being that he is the only Polish-speaking business lawyer in that region. That means he is far more likely to have the Polish speaking businesses in his town as clients, as well as many other businesses.

Need

In order to succeed in a market, there must be a need for you and your product or service. A lot of business owners, or inventors, have a fantastic product that nobody wants. The concept of creating the market is a rarity and definitely not the task of a small business. Companies such as Da Beers were able to create a new market because they have billions of dollars to do so. Beyond just the money, it also takes years to create a new market.

Tip: Viral marketing to educate the population isn't a worthwhile strategy. It has nearly a 100% failure rate. A viral advertisement isn't something you can plan.

Story: Our firm had a potential client come in and show us his proposed business plan. He allocated $0 for marketing for the first year. When asked about the marketing budget, he responded that it was fine because he was going to do viral marketing. His company has not been successful, and we elected not to represent him until he came up with a more realistic marketing strategy.

You've already listed which intrinsic needs your products or services satisfy, but now we need to make sure that your demographic has the need that requires satisfying.

Not only does your product need to satisfy an intrinsic need, there must also be the need in the demographic you're targeting. If half your town are accountants, there is not a need for another accountant, unless, of course, you're offering something different for which there is a need for. Finding a need is easy, but defining the need and recording that need is harder and very important in this process. It is this need that you will exploit and use to get you customers.

A colleague of mine does sports massage therapy. He realized there was a need to have simpler billing practices and more frequent sessions. Therefore, he created a flat monthly cost for as many sessions as is needed. It was as simple as that, and his business is doing very well. It's doing as well as it is because there were several needs and he filled those needs with his business. Fulfilling those needs also sets him apart.

[ ] Step 36 - For each product or service that has the list of needs they solve, determine if those needs are the needs of your demographic. If they're not, remove that product or service from your list.

Market Size

You will want to analyze the market size in two aspects. (1) The number and size of the purchasers and (2) the number and size of the competitors.

You want to analyze the number and size of the purchasers first. Your market can be between just 1 person up to 7 billion people, so it's best to narrow that down. Are you selling to a one purchaser market, like to the United States government? Or, are you selling something like bread that has billions of consumers? This will change how much room there is for you in the market. It also helps determine who you need to research to determine if there's a need. If you have a market of one, you can ask if they would want what you offer before you make it. Larger markets need a little more market research.

Next, you'll want to analyze the number and size of your competitors. You're looking to see if there are already too many competitors in the market that would make it very hard for you to profit on what you do. You also want to look at the size of the competitors. If you decided to start selling diamonds, you're in for some trouble. There is one major diamond seller and they tend to put every other diamond seller out of business because they're huge and have the resources and ability to do that. Going head-to-head against major fashion retailers is also typically a bad idea. Jeans is not a market to get into. It isn't saturated, but the major retailers hold such strong ties and strong brand that they make it nearly impossible to break into the market.

The size of the competitors also shows you how cheaply they can make the product if you're selling a product, or how efficiently they can brand themselves or market in ways that would harm your company's chances of success.

One good way to tell if your product market is oversaturated is if you cannot produce the product for less than the price of a comparable product in the market. As markets become saturated, variable costs and price become increasingly close, dissolving the profit margin of everyone in the market. Also, if your profit margin multiplied by the number of sales cannot cover your overhead, it's overly saturated. You'll either need to find a way to cut costs or differentiate what you're offering.

Markets that have fewer barriers to entry and are easier to get into will have lower profit margins because of this, or they will have lower profit margins sometime in the future. Keep that in mind. The harder it is to get into the market, the better the margins can be because the market is less efficient with fewer competitors.

[ ] Step 37 - Write down the number of potential customers you have.

[ ] Step 38 - Write down the number of competitors you will have.

[ ] Step 39 - Write down the market share of each of the competitors, if that's applicable.

Marketing and Sales

Now that you have information on your branding approach, the market, your demographic and the need you are focusing on filling, you can start creating a marketing and sales strategy.

[ ] Step 40 - To create this strategy, start by writing down every single marketing idea you have, whether good or bad. This is your mind dump and should take you at least an hour.

Feel free to gather others for this because this is your creative portion. No idea is too dumb.

Tip: Think of this portion as the "come up with stupid ideas" portion of the planning. Sometimes it helps to think of the most outlandish marketing ideas because those spark legitimate ideas.

Every marketing idea comes with a lot of descriptive characteristics. You have costs, return on investment, and importantly, the values the marketing idea represents. Each different idea showcases a different feel to it. For example, charitable work exhibits kindness, helpfulness, dedication to the community and many more similar values.

[ ] Step 41 - Next to each marketing idea, list the top five values this idea exemplifies.

As we illustrated above, each idea also comes with costs. Costs can be monetary, time, or any other thing you have to give up in order to conduct the marketing idea.

[ ] Step 42 - List the expected cost in money, time and any other costs that you may associate with it, like the inability to do another type of marketing.

Your ideas may be good, bad, or somewhere in between. At this stage, a good idea is one that matches many of your company values and has a cost you can afford. Bad ideas are ones that either do not match your company's values, or the idea is one you cannot afford with your current cash flow or time availability.

[ ] Step 43 - Go through your list of marketing ideas and classify them as "good," "bad values," "bad costs," or "uncertain." Move the different classifications into different lists with these headings. If you don't have any ideas marked as "good," start the listing process all over again.

Hopefully you are pleasantly surprised by the ideas you have in your good list. Those in your bad costs column are a good list to pull from later.

Yes, many of your ideas listed are probably pretty bad ideas, but do not get rid of them completely, as they may be useful later. Instead, we're keeping these ideas in a separate list that we can reference later.

Tip: No one will know your company values unless you market toward them. If you value charitable giving, to keep with our example, you should advertise when you do charitable things.

Every marketing idea also has expected payout. The payout is much harder to predict without having done the idea in the past. Marketing firms and more established companies know what to expect from their marketing efforts. You're going to have to make educated guesses here.

[ ] Step 44 -   Using the best possible predictions you can make, list the expected payout from each marketing idea. This is your return on investment (ROI) for the marketing project. You can also list this as a percent with the idea by dividing the return by the investment and subtracting one.

Your singular project should look something like this now:
Volunteering at Wills for Heroes
Cost: $0 plus 8 hours
Return: $500   ROI: $62.50 / hour plus reputation.
Values: Charitable, Kindness, Commitment to Military, Expertise, Commitment to Family and Children

[ ] Step 45 -   If any of your items have specific rules for how the hours or money must be spread out, include those rules in your descriptions. For example, if your Wills for Heroes requires two hours contacting press at least three weeks prior to the event, include those two hours at least three weeks prior rule in your description.

Marketing Optimization

Many people get a list of marketing ideas and jump right in with what they believe to be the best option. We've got a better way. A few minutes of planning can give you savings of significant money and hundreds of hours every year. There are software solutions that can do this as well, but for our purposes, the manual way will suffice for now.

> [ ] Step 46 - Create a cash flow diagram that also has your available time. Make this diagram a timeline starting at the present and going at least one year in the future, preferably two or three. Put in moments where your money or time availability changes because of other items that are more necessary than this marketing.

Your timeline should be incredibly long and would likely be more useful using some sort of spreadsheet program. You want to make the units of measurement equal to the timeframe for paying and receiving payments. You cannot fail, however, by breaking it down into days.

Tip: Check out our website www.checkmarkstartup.com for a downloadable spreadsheet.

A sample beginning of a timeline looks like this:

	11/1/16	11/2/16	11/3/16
Available Marketing Hours	5	3	4
Committed Marketing Hours	0	0	0
Marketing Hours Remaining	5	3	4
Available Marketing Dollars	$0	$5	$10
Committed Marketing Dollars	$0	$0	$10
Marketing Dollars Remaining	$0	$5	$0

This is, of course, only one way of making the timeline and may not work for you. It is set up in a daily fashion so that it can be more specific. There's something lost when you do monthly or weekly basis because you may have points during the month with negative cash flow that evens out at the end of the month. Therefore, making your timeline in a daily system makes it safer. Absent some type of credit or investment, your current cash cannot go negative, and your time does not magically increase.

Tip: Time resets every day, but your money can accumulate. Keep that in mind for your planning purposes.

With this timeline, you can see where you have the cash flow and available time to utilize for expansion and working on building your business opposed to the necessary items such as doing the business work you must do. Having both of these variables on your timeline will allow you to see where your time and money are scarce, so you do not run out of either at any point.

As some things take only time or only money, you can mix and match your strategies in order to most efficiently use your time and money. If you're out of money but have a lot of time, it is a good idea to do things that require only time and no money whereas if you're out of time but the money is free-flowing, you should consider strategies that use only money and no time.

[ ] Step 47 - Start putting your strategies in the spreadsheet, starting with those items that have the highest ROI that you can afford. If you're using our provided spreadsheet, you can simply add each item to the table and see the effects on the cash and time flow diagram. You should never see red.

Detailed Marketing Plan (Not Implementation)

Before spending a single dollar on marketing, you should develop this comprehensive marketing plan. Spending many hours developing this plan or even money to have someone else develop it will save you thousands of dollars in misspent money once you begin implementing, not to mention preventing stalled or even reversed efforts in growing your company.

[ ] Step 48 - Write out the plan items in the order they occur in your spreadsheet you've just created. This can look like a daily calendar or any other format that works well for you. Put as much detail as you can here so you'll understand what you meant significantly down the road.

Tip: This is also an opportunity to combine any portions that you can combine. For example: while you're researching local reporters for one project, you can also research local publication awards.

The reason a marketing plan saves you money is because you can find the optimal use of your money and time before sending your company in one direction.

[ ] Step 49 - Look at your plan and ensure that the balance of the values you're representing is how you want your company to be viewed. If it isn't the balance you want, go back to the spreadsheet and start including activities that represent your company's values.

Pricing

Pricing is different from value. Pricing must be directly related to value, but it must also be optimized so that you have enough profit margin to make it worthwhile to support you and your monetary value of your own time. Look at your competitor's prices and determine if (a) you can make a profit at that price or (b) if you're distinguished enough that you can charge a different price

[ ] Step 50 - List competitor prices for all of your products and services, if there are any, and list what distinguishes you from these competitors.

If you're not distinguished and cannot profit at that price, you shouldn't try to sell that product or service. Instead, pivot your strategy to lower costs or create a more valuable, distinguishable, product.

Generally, new players in a market need higher quality or lower price; otherwise, they cannot gain the traction necessary in the marketplace.

Tip: There are a lot of ways to distinguish yourself. Better marketing, higher quality, easier to use, and more would all apply.

Profit Maximization

To determine your pricing, you should try to maximize the profit generated at each particular price point. To do this, you should consider how you bill for your product or service. There are several ways to bill. Generally, the higher your price, and the earlier a customer has to pay, the fewer clients you will get.

Commission

Mostly in service industries, but also available in some products, you can bill on a commission-based model. Whether you're saving a person money or getting them more money, you can bill on a percent of the money gained or saved.

For example, many personal injury lawyers will bill on a commission basis for cases. This helps their clients because it doesn't cost any money up front. When your clients have a cash flow issue, this may be a better solution; however, it hurts your cash flow, and it may not be viable if it means your effective rate is very low.

[ ] Step 51 - Is a commission based solution possible for you? If so, what do you see as the pros and cons?

Per Item

Billing on a per item basis is the most common method for billing, especially in product lines. In this method, you set a specific price for each item and sell it at that price no matter who buys, how long it takes or how much benefit the customer receives. This is how retail stores work.

Subscription

Subscriptions are a method of billing that is becoming increasingly common. Software, especially, sees subscriptions on a regular basis. What this means is that your customer pays a specific price over a period of time.

Example: If you've registered for paid antivirus software, you're using a subscription, paying between $5 and $100+ per month until you cancel your subscription.

The subscription model is especially useful when you are providing a service over time or a license to use some good or intellectual property.

Tip: A lawyer "retainer" can either mean a subscription or an account you must fill which is slowly billed to before you're required to refill the account.

[ ] Step 52 -   Write down any products or services that can fit into this model.

À la Carte

À la carte is a method of billing that starts with a per item billing model, but with add-on items that the customer can purchase in order to add only the value they want to add. This provides the customer the opportunity to maximize the value they receive for the price they're willing to pay. Think of adding a side dish at a restaurant when it is per item plus à la carte, or getting a smoothie at your gym as an add on to your monthly subscription.

Per Hour (Hourly)

Per hour billing is common in service industries. In this billing model, you would bill for your time and add in expenses as you incur them. In certain circumstances, this is the fairest way to be compensated for your work. However, because this billing model is unpredictable, you may find many of your customers do not appreciate the uncertainty of this billing model.

Especially in situations where you cannot accurately predict how long it will take for you to complete the service you are about to perform, this may be the best option for you. Professional services such as doctors, lawyers, and accountants typically bill in this way.

[ ] Step 53 - Using what you know about billing, write down the billing strategy or combination of strategies you will be using in your business.

Tip: Keep It Simple Silly. Any confusion in billing practices will lessen how many customers you will obtain. With the same price, you will have more customers in a simple billing practice than a complex one.

Choosing a Price

As mentioned before, a price needs to reflect value, but it also must be profitable. With any product or service you are selling, you should start with your COGS, or cost of goods sold. The COGS represents the various costs that go directly into that product or service. For example, if you're selling a good, the COGS is the cost of the parts and labor to make that good, but not the overhead lighting, insurances, etc. that do not change directly based on the number of goods you produce.

Choosing a price isn't an easy process. There's a lot of math that goes into it, and at the end of the day, you're basically guessing and testing. The economic principles that go into choosing a price are great for several years after the fact, and the market, as a whole, will help determine price; however, that doesn't help you at the outset of this process.

What you need to do is make the best educated guess you can.

Start with COGS and then make a determination of how many of each product or service you would be able to sell at a given price and then choose the price that maximizes profit.

Tip: A/B testing, or doing a little bit of market research, can help you determine the appropriate price.

[ ] Step 54 - List the price you've chosen, or prices, for your products or services based on your educated guess. If you have more than one potential strategy, list the prices for all and then choose the method that you believe would be the most profitable.

CHAPTER 7 - OTHER BUSINESS NEEDS

Your product or service, marketing, team and mission statement don't make up the entirety of your company. There are other needs your business has that mostly fall into the administrative category. These typically aren't income producing, but are either necessary by law or are otherwise beneficial for you.

Real Estate

Real estate is the office space, manufacturing space or any other building or land that is owned or leased by your business.

Tip: You shouldn't own or lease any business property in your own name.

Own

Owning real estate means that you've bought it. You can buy land, buy an existing structure, build a new structure, or buy part of an existing structure. Owning the space has the advantage of being an asset of the company; however, it usually has the disadvantage of a larger upfront cost.

If you own real estate, you're also responsible for taxes, maintenance and utilities.

Lease

A lease is the right to use a piece of real estate for a specific period of time. The advantage of a lease is that you're looking at lower upfront cost, but you're not building equity in a piece of property and are subject to the rules and regulations of the landlord.

You can generally get a lease as a new company, whereas getting a loan as a brand new company for construction is nearly impossible without a co-signor.

> [ ] Step 55 - If you require, or believe you may require, real estate, write down your requirements, expected benefits, and expected costs. If real estate isn't a concern, skip the steps in this section, but read the rest of this section nonetheless. Do some research or contact a commercial realtor to get a better idea of costs for your requirements.

The balance here must be between the cost and commitment you must give up versus the benefit the real estate would provide. The benefit may also include compliance with the law or as a necessity for your business.

Tip: Having a location builds credibility, but it's not the only way to build credibility.

> [ ] Step 56 - Compare the costs and benefits from before and determine if you can afford and/or want real estate at this time. If you decide you do want real estate at this time, include the requirements, costs and benefits in your business plan under the subheading "Real Estate."

Insurance

Insurance is a way to limit your liability in specific instances that are generally outside the control of the party that is insured. Everyone has heard of auto insurance which protects you in the case of a car accident, but it doesn't protect you if you choose to take a wrecking ball to your own car.

Business insurances work in a similar way and the policies vary as far as what they cover. Every company should have at least a general liability policy, which will cover bodily injury, property damage and, many times, theft.

There are also Errors & Omissions (E&O) insurance, which covers negligence in your professional duties, such as for accountants in their performance of their duties. This is very similar to malpractice insurance, except that malpractice insurance is for very specific industries like doctors and lawyers. Anyone can obtain errors & omissions insurance.

Tip: Business insurances never cover intentional acts.

[ ] Step 57 - Call or email your local insurance representative and get quotes for general liability insurance and errors & omissions insurance (if applicable). Do Not Buy Yet, but tell him or her that you will be setting up a company soon. Your insurance provider will have a better idea of what limits you need and if you need the E&O insurance at all.

Tip: In some states, proper insurance coverage is a requirement to keep your limited liability protection through an LLC or Corporation.

Capital Equipment

Most companies require capital equipment to get started. This equipment ranges from a laptop to manufacturing equipment and everything in between.

You can provide the equipment you already own as the capital equipment, but you should sell, lease, or transfer the equipment to your company once it is legally formed, so you can receive the beneficial tax treatment. A CPA or tax attorney can advise you which route is best for your specific circumstance.

If you do contribute used items, keep in mind that used equipment are generally worth less than new equipment, and any valuation you give your contributed or sold equipment should reflect what someone would pay for it in its current condition.

Capital equipment does not include inventory or office supplies. Those things are covered later.

[ ] Step 58 - Make a list of all capital equipment your company needs, including why you need each piece of equipment and its current value, if you've transferred it from you personally.

[ ] Step 59 - List in your business plan any capital equipment you have and equipment you still need to obtain.

Education

Sometimes, it is necessary to obtain some education or skills training as a part of your business. This can include things like becoming certified in a particular field, learning a new software package or language, and more.

Ongoing education to become better in your field or education hours that are require as part of a profession should not be included here. This section is for education that is necessary to provide the products or services you've listed earlier.

[ ] Step 60 - List any education that is necessary to provide your products or services and their associated costs in your business plan under Education or Skills Training.

Software

It is tough to have a business in today's world without the use of software. This section isn't included in every business plan, but I believe it is very important to figure out early to avoid any issues getting set up later.

At a minimum, you will likely need an email program and word processor, but these are some of the categories of software you may

want to look into:
- Accounting and billing
- Voice over IP phone
- Calendaring
- Spreadsheet or other statistical analysis software
- Software that is specific to your industry

[ ] Step 61 - Make a list of any software you will need and the anticipated cost and add this list of software to your business plan.

[ ] Step 62 - Spend a few minutes getting used to using the software you've chosen to use.

Inventory/Supplies

Not every business has inventory or supplies, but most do. If you're in a business that has no inventory or supplies, feel free to skip these steps.

[ ] Step 63 - Make a list of inventory or supplies that you require to obtain prior to opening and any inventory you would need for the first three months.

Keep in mind that office supplies like staples can be very necessary, yet not thought of until you need them. In my law firm, it was binder clips that we ran out of and needed them suddenly. Now, we probably won't run out for 10 years.

[ ] Step 64 - Create a system for checking your inventory or supplies and how you will reorder.

Tip: The automation provided by software solutions for managing inventory and reordering supplies can be one of best time saving solutions you can utilize.

CHAPTER 8 - BUDGET

Expected Expenses

In your business plan, you will want include all of your expected expenses for the first few years. The closer the anticipated expense is to the present, the more detailed the list should be, but you'll want to be as accurate as possible so that you have a good picture of how much money you will need and how much you will need to generate.

This list, combined with your expected revenue list, will help guide you on investment decisions and help you with your budgets in upcoming years. Appendix II is a good starter list for costs.

Using this list, you will begin to generate a cash flow diagram. In early companies, cash flow will rule what you can and cannot do.

[ ] Step 65 - Write down a list of all your expenses, separating them into reoccurring and onetime expenses.

There is also a huge difference between required expenses and desired expenses. For each required expense, there isn't much you can do to limit them. If you can reduce any of your expenses yet keep the same value, you should, of course, do that. For each of your desired expenses, you'll have to analyze what value they bring compared to their cost (Rate of Return). The higher percentage rate of return, the better, but not all returns are immediately measurable.

[ ] Step 66 - Using your list of expenses, classify each item as a required expense or desired expense.

There is actually an advanced analysis you can do to determine which desired expenditures you should make, but a lot of it is common sense. You're limited by cash flow and want to increase value as much as possible.

In order to maintain your cash flow, you may not be able to choose everything, but you should still keep the ones you're unable to do in a sub list. If you have extra cash flow beyond what you expected or more cash flow in the future, you'll likely want to branch into other ideas as well.

[ ] Step 67 - Look at your budget that you've created before and make adjustments knowing what you know now, including the marketing costs and capital equipment you need to buy.

Once again, generally if your cash drops below $0 in the first twelve months, you need additional funding or to cut expenses somehow, but we'll do this after the revenues have been added.

Expected Revenues

Expected Revenues is the other side of the coin. Your revenue is hard to predict, but the prediction also sets itself up to be the goals you use. It is better to be conservative with your expected revenues so you do not overcommit your company's money to things you might not be able to afford. The revenue is the cash flow you need in order to determine which expenses you're able to utilize in your plan.

[ ] Step 68 - Using the same cash flow spreadsheet you've entered your expenses on, include your expected revenues.

As you start getting revenue, you will keep updating this, and over time, you'll be able to better predict where the revenue will actually fall in each upcoming month. Keeping this as accurate as possible is important for helping accurately determine which projects and expenses you're able to afford.

If you're able to create products or services that generate predictable cash flow, these will make your budgeting significantly easier.

Tip: You can separate revenue into multiple categories to make it easier to view and predict.

COGS

If you sell a product, cost of goods sold (COGS) is one of the most important calculations you could have. You will need to know exactly how much it costs to create each product. This includes material, labor, percent of overhead (if a dedicated manufacturing facility), and anything else that goes into each product. There will likely be ways to reduce the price through materials or quantity, so including this analysis is also very important.

The cost of goods sold analysis helped you determine what price you can sell your product for at retail and wholesale prices earlier. It also is critical for determining how much quantity you need to sell in order to reach your revenue prediction. If you've kept great records on marketing procedures, you will then also be able to predict return on marketing and will know how much money and time you will need to spend in certain areas to reach the revenue predictions you've made.

Services also have a cost of goods sold analysis, but it is called cost of revenue. This includes any costs directly attributed to the provision of a service. For example, a massage parlor must clean each table after use as well as use candles and oils during the massage. They will also have to clean the towels and provide appointment cards for each and every appointment. These expenses that occur with each massage are the cost of revenue for that massage parlor.

[ ] Step 69 - Make sure that your expenses and revenue match up appropriately with the proper cost of goods sold for the revenue you are predicting.

CHAPTER 9 - EXECUTIVE SUMMARY

The first page of the content of your business plan is your executive summary; however, it is typically written as one of the last items. We do this because you cannot write a summary of the company until you've written the full plan for the company.

Your executive summary should include a shorter description of your products or services, your marketing plan, any investments or capital you need to raise in the beginning, and a summary of the goals for the company. A good executive summary is usually 1-2 pages and contains just enough detail that a person can understand what your company does and how it will make money, but the reader will need to read the specific sections to get any detailed information regarding these areas.

Description

The executive summary starts with a very brief description of your company, including the name, location, and products or services offered.

[ ] Step 70 - Write down the planned name of your company, city and state where it is located in, and a short description of your products or services.

Note: You can change this later as with everything in your business plan.

[ ] Step 71 - Take the information you wrote in the last step and turn it into a one sentence intro.

Example: Law Plus Plus is a law firm in Durham, NC that offers general legal representation for small to mid-sized companies in the Raleigh-Durham area, including contracts, formations, employment, and litigation legal services.

[ ] Step 72 - If there are multiple products or services that your company offers, put these in the next 1-2 sentences.

Example: Specifically, we provide contract drafting and reviewing, company formations, partnership agreements, trademarks, employment transactional and dispute management, and business litigation representation.

Uniqueness

The next couple of sentences will outline what sets your company apart from other companies, or what makes your company desirable. Refer to the earlier step where you defined what makes your company unique.

[ ] Step 73 - Write the remainder of the first paragraph by illustrating what makes your company unique.

Example: We offer flat rate prices and easy to understand subscription models, so companies can have a clear understanding of what they are paying for and the value they receive.

Need

Your first paragraph should also include what you require to get to where you want to be. If you need an investment, you want to list this here. If you don't require investment, you can save the part about costs and growth until later.

[ ] Step 74 - If your business requires an investment or loan, put how much and what that will do for the company in the final sentence of the first paragraph.

Products/Services

In the next paragraph, you want to describe how your company provides the products or services it does, and how that benefits the customers.

[ ] Step 75 - Write the paragraph about how your company provides the products or services, including the benefit these have to your customers. If needed, you can make this multiple paragraphs.

Making the Sales

The final paragraph should include how you intend to reach your customers, and how you plan on growing your company. You've already written most of this in your marketing plan, but now you're summarizing it in a paragraph so it can be quickly understood.

[ ] Step 76 - Write the paragraph about how you plan on reaching your customers, and how you plan to grow the company.

It is a personal decision, but you may want to include some of your longer term goals, values, and/or mission statement in the executive summary as well. My personal preference is to include both the mission statement and the longest term goals in my mission statement.

Tip: You can include anything you want in your executive summary. It's a combination between a summary of your plan and a business pitch.

[ ] Step 77 - Reading through your executive summary, include anything else you may feel would add value, while keeping this section brief. Fix any typos or grammar mistakes as well.

Readability

A good executive summary is one that can be read and understood by someone who is not familiar at all with your industry or your company. It should give your reader an image of what the company does, how it does it better than others, and how it plans on growing.

[ ] Step 78 - Pretending you know nothing about your business, reread and edit your executive summary to ensure that anyone could understand what your business does.

Tip: Give your executive summary to a friend or family member who knows nothing about your industry to get valuable feedback.

Although this section is much shorter than the other sections, it is not unimportant. If you're writing the summary only for yourself, this helps you craft your elevator speech for when you're looking to make sales.

If, however, you're looking for investment, this is the very first thing that an investor reads; therefore, it is incredibly important. Failure to put the right amount of time up front can result in automatic rejection from banks or investors, or a significantly larger amount of time later.

Tip: Never lie, and never be overly optimistic. If you list something unachievable, your audience will immediately pick up on that.

CHAPTER 10 - PROCESSES AND PROFESSIONALS

Before you get buried in work, you'll want to set up some systems to make things more efficient for you later. In order to ensure you remember the systems when you actually need them, it's important to write them down in your business plan for later reference. As with the entire business plan, these can, and should, change as you become more efficient or as your process changes to meet changing needs or goals.

Tip: These expected processes will later be called the standard operating procedure, which we will cover later.

You should outline your processes in such a way that if you were hit by the proverbial bus, someone else would be able to do your job. Since you're likely not going to be hit by a bus, the real purpose behind these written processes is for you to expend little to no mental energy executing them. Most of your mental energy should be put into developing new strategies for growing your business or actually working on your business.

Any place where you have repetition is a chance to save mental energy by creating a system that takes care of the repetition or remembering for you. For example, you shouldn't try to keep track of all of your clients in your head. Create a system for that, preferably computerized and searchable by many terms.

[ ] Step 79 - Write down a list of tasks that you envision repeating pretty regularly in your business.

Don't forget to include items in your list such as how you bill clients, how bills get paid, quality control measures, and any marketing systems you may have.

Writing down your systems is also crucial if you ever plan on hiring others to take over certain aspects of your business. With clear written instructions, you greatly decrease the cost and amount of energy you must spend training your new hire.

[ ] Step 80 - For each item in your above list, create a step-by-step guide to completing that task. Put in as much detail as possible, and if there are hyperlinks or online resources, make this guide electronic.

Tip: Using a tool like Google Docs for your expected processes makes it so you can access it from anywhere, share with your colleagues and track changes you've made over time.

Your calendar is also a system that is a must have. Never rely on your mind to keep track of every appointment. This will drive you crazy, even if you have very few appointments. There's no reason your mind should be wasted on tasks like these when it can be used for higher level thinking.

[ ] Step 81 - Choose a calendar program you will use and make sure you can access it on all of your devices, add events easily, and include reoccurring events. Add any events or meetings you already have.

The book "Getting Things Done: The Art of Stress-Free Productivity" by David Allen provides a good way to think about freeing up your mental energy and ensuring everything on your to-do list gets done. The less you have to remember, the more efficient your mind.

Professional Team

Your professional team is part of your business plan, as there will be points, especially early on, that you will have to call on your professional team. This is different than what is discussed in the "Building the Team" chapter later on because your professional team are people that provide you much needed advice on running your business from a foundational standpoint versus those people you bring in to help you run your business or grow your business.

Every company needs a CPA, attorney, business coach, and financial advisor. Together, these professionals provide you with the foundational support you need to create and run a business. Not only will these people help keep you out of trouble, they'll also be able to guide you so that growth is met with far fewer obstacles.

[ ] Step 82 - Think about who you want as your company's attorney, CPA, business coach, and financial advisor. If you already have one of any of these, list them in your business plan under the Professional Team header.

Each professional does not have to be a different person. For example, your attorney can be your business coach, if your attorney offers that service. It is, however, important to choose professionals you can trust and work with. It helps to choose someone who takes the time to know the intimate details of your business, so that they are able to better advise you.

Tip: Don't pick a friend or a family member as any of these professionals if you can avoid it. You want this person to be able to remove the emotion from any feedback, so that you can receive the best advice possible, also keeping in mind friends and family may be more valuable as emotional support.

If you don't have all of your professional team listed, be sure to do that as soon as possible, as we'll be referencing these people later in the book.

Tip: If you have one of your professional team, he or she will likely be able to refer qualified and trusted individuals to fill the other roles.

CHAPTER 11 - COVER YOUR EXPENSES

Initial Financial Contributions

Businesses cost money to get up and running. Even the least capital intensive service industry will require some level of financial contribution to get started, at least to pay for things such as paper for bookkeeping, writing utensils, office space or gas for the car, as well as the formation and license fees.

Tip: Appendix II has some sample startup costs.

To prepare, you've already created your cash flow spreadsheet. If, at any point, you have a negative amount in cash, you will need to cut costs, increase revenue, or have some sort of outside investment. It depends on your industry, but generally, you should look 1-2 years out without relying on any cash flow that is not guaranteed.

Using the cash flow spreadsheet you've previously created and the determination of how you will finance your company that you made in Chapter 2, we're now going to create a plan for getting funding.

[ ] Step 83 - If you need additional money to start your business, research how you would go about getting funding in your area and record the steps you would need to take.

It is okay to reevaluate your source of funding at any time until you're contractually obligated. It is best to choose the most advantageous strategy from the start, but sometimes changing midway through is cheaper than continuing on a course that is inappropriate for your needs.

Tip: Any research time is a sunk cost. You shouldn't consider time spent when determining whether it would be best to switch.

[ ] Step 84 - Using your research, create a list of milestones you will need to complete in order to get funding. Add due dates for your milestones based on your reasonable expectations for when your steps can be completed.

At the stage we're in now, it is far cheaper to switch plans than if you've already accepted investor or bank money. Once you've accepted these, you're contractually bound by a lot more terms, and you may even have personal obligations.

[ ] Step 85 - After completing your milestones and deadlines, either commit to those deadlines or switch sources of funding and start this research and milestone process over.

Tip: A sample milestone list for each funding source can be found in Appendix III, but they will require more detail than provided.

Many times, you require a combination of more than one funding source. This is fine as long as you are not prevented from doing so by any of your earlier funders.

Tip: If anything ever feels sketchy, or you're uncomfortable with a funding route, you should walk away. This is a moment to really trust your instincts because if you misstep, you can either get into a lot of trouble or end up hurting your company.

CHAPTER 12 - BUSINESS PLAN AS A LIVING DOCUMENT

Measure Twice, Cut Once

This is the part of the book where you put everything from your business plan together, but this doesn't mean your business plan is done. Your business plan is a living document; it should change as your circumstances change, as your plans change and as you receive more accurate information. You should be reading and adapting your business plan at least monthly.

[ ] Step 86 - Add your goals into the goals section of the business plan.

Your goals will also change from time to time. As these change, you should revisit the business plan. The plan itself should be your default location when looking for your long term business goals.

[ ] Step 87 - Add your company values and mission statement to the values and mission statement section of the business plan.

You should still have several areas incomplete in your business plan. Don't worry, we'll address those further down the road.

Because your plans change frequently, you should commit to

reviewing your plan every month for the first 3 years. During these reviews, you want to look at your values and your mission statement. Ask yourself: Have your actions been furthering your mission and if you have been placing your values at the forefront of every decision?

After looking at your values and mission, you want to look at your goals. Have you been working toward these goals? Do any of them need to be updated or changed?

If you've made any changes to your plans during the previous month, you also want to update your business plan sections that have changed. One of the most frequent changes is your marketing plan.

[ ] Step 88 -   Put in your calendar a specific date and time
every month that you're going to read through your
business plan, paying very close attention to your goals.

Tip: Don't be afraid to print off your business plan. It is easy to gloss over electronic media.

When you're going over your business plan, the most important thing is being honest with yourself. It is common to be too easy or too hard on yourself with goals and following plans. Your goals should be measurable, so you have a way to compare your current results with where you want to be. When doing these, it is a good idea to document your current standings.

Tip: Use your business coach or a colleague to go over your business plan with you. This greatly increases your accountability.

PART 3
FOUNDATION

CHAPTER 13 - LEGAL FORMATION

The first legal step to having a company is forming that company. This process is creatively named formation.

Do You Need to Form a Company?

Do you even need to form a company? Would it benefit you at all to have a legal recognition as a separate entity?

It's a bit of a misnomer to suggest that you aren't forming a company when you don't file papers with your state. No matter what type of company you choose, if you have business activities, you've formed a company. If you didn't file articles with the state, you have a sole proprietorship (with one owner) or partnership (if you have more than one owner).

The most common types of entities are Sole Proprietorships, Corporations, Partnerships, and Limited Liability Companies. There are a significant number of other types available in the United States, but we're focusing on these.

Corporations were invented over 400 years ago in order to separate individual liability from company liability. This was the first development that separated ownership from liability. This separation of ownership from liability is a great reason to form a company other than a sole proprietorship or partnership.

The default is that everyone who is running a business should form a separate legal entity. Personally assuming the entire weight of the business liability is dangerous, especially in startups that may be borrowing money or taking additional risk.

What it means to have personal liability is to be personally responsible for all of the debts and financial liabilities of the company. This includes things like loans, contracts, lawsuits and any debts the company incurs.

Forming a separate legal entity puts this risk almost completely at the company level. You can only lose the money you've already put into the company when the company has to pay its liabilities.

The profits are still yours, but the taxation on the money the company receives may be different depending on the type of company you choose.

So, why wouldn't you want to form a separate legal entity? If it doesn't make financial sense to do so, you may decide it's worth the risk. If your company makes less than $200 per year, you're looking at earning less than the annual report costs. Many localities also have annual business licenses, not to mention the initial cost to form the company. Additionally, if the biggest portion of your liability is going to affect you regardless of entity type, it may be your best choice to not form a legal entity.

Professionals who need malpractice insurance are in this boat, but still form companies for the tax benefits and the protection from contractual liabilities. This chart helps demonstrate the different types of liabilities your company can face and whether they're business or personal liabilities:

	Business	Personal
Professional acts (Lawyer, doctor, etc.)	X	X
Contracts with no cosigner (Leases, credit cards, loans, customer disputes, etc.)	X	
Contracts with you cosigning	X	X
Employees	X	
Real estate liability (Slip and falls)	X	
Intentional acts by you	X	X
Government regulations	X	Sometimes
Taxes	X	Some

If you have more than one person in the company, you will want to form a separate legal entity because when you go into business with another person without forming a separate legal entity, you've formed a general partnership, usually just called a partnership for short. In a general partnership, there is no limited liability. In fact, there is increased liability because each partner in the partnership is fully liable for the acts of the company. Because each partner is an owner of the company, they typically have full reign to act on behalf of the company however they'd like. Therefore, you'd be responsible for any acts, contracts, lawsuits, etc. caused by your partner.

Picking a Name

The first step to creating a legal entity is choosing your company's name. This is a creative part, so this book is of little help. The objective of coming up with a name can be either creative, descriptive or a combination of both.

Google is a creative name and not descriptive, and it has one of the strongest brand names around. We all know the advantages of creating a very strong brand, but it takes more time and effort to build that brand reputation.

A name such as The Law Office of Richard Bobholz would be purely descriptive. The advantage to the descriptive name is that people already know a fair bit about your company just from the name.

A name such as Pegasus Law Group would be a combination of the two, unless of course the name of the owner was Pegasus, or they practiced the field of Pegasus Law.

[ ] Step 89 - Write down a list of at least 10 names you'd want for your company.

What's in a name?

Every name you come up with has some connotation to it. There's a reason heavy metal bands all have similar sounding names. You're going to want to pick a name that appropriately conveys the message you're looking to convey to your customers and the public.

[ ] Step 90 - List the values you believe each name exemplifies, if any.

Tip: Completely made-up words are a blank canvas for assigning values whereas borrowed words tend to come with connotation.

There are some requirements when it comes to naming, and we'll explore some of these now.

Search Google

After you've made your list, you want to search Google, or some other major search engine. You want to make sure that you can end up high on the search ratings and not be confused with other listings or products that sound similar to your company name.

Funny Note: I had a client debating names and found the one that they loved. It was available everywhere, but once we searched the internet for it, we found out it was a common slang term for a sex act. The entire first couple of pages of Google were talking about this act, so we knew this client would have an impossibly hard time using that name.

All the listings on the first page of the search engine will affect your brand, so it's important that you find terms that do not go contrary to your message and values. Even if you had no idea that this name meant something else, your customers will be seeing these other results every time they search for you, and your brand will be damaged.

If you find your name being used commonly in business, it may be trademarked, but we will discuss that in the USPTO section.

[ ] Step 91 - Use Google, or another major search engine, and search for each name idea you had, with expected variations or standalone portions of the name.

For example, if your name is Pegasus Landscaping and World Hunger Elimination Fund, search the whole phrase, Pegasus Landscaping, World Hunger Elimination Fund, World Hunger Elimination, Pegasus Hunger, Landscaping and World Huger, Pegasus World Hunger Elimination Fund, Elimination Fund, and common misspellings of all of these. If you think people may search for any other combination, search that too.

Reserved Words

In every state and through the federal government, there are words you are not allowed to use. For example, you are not allowed to use the word "Insurance" unless you've been approved to sell or provide insurance products.

[ ] Step 92 - Check with your state to see which words are not allowed.

In North Carolina, the statutorily prohibited words are Bank, Banker, Banking, Trust, Mutual, Cooperative, Co-op, Insurance, Engineer, Engineering, Architect, Architecture, Architectural, Surveyor, Survey, Surveying, Certified Public Accountant and abbreviations of such, Wholesale, Realtor, or curse words.

[ ] Step 93 - Compare the names on your list to ensure that these impermissible words are not included, eliminating any that will not be permitted.

Tip: If you're planning on expanding into another state, be sure to check the impermissible words in the other states you're looking to move into.

Misleading

Your name is not allowed to be misleading. For example, you cannot describe yourself as a bookkeeping service if you offer dance instruction services. This is important for both legal requirements and branding.

Tip: Any time you trick someone into using your service, you've broken the trust you have with the community.

Intent to Deceive

You cannot form a company with a name that is intended to deceive. For example, you cannot make a company 13rooks Brothers and place it next to Brooks Brothers with spacing between the 1 and the 3 so little that it looks like a 'B.'

[ ] Step 94 - Looking at your list of names, eliminate any that are misleading or deceptive.

Professional Services

Most states include prohibitions on using names that say you offer professional services like legal, medical, engineering, architectural and others without permission from the licensing board for that professional service. The names may also have to be approved by the licensing board and permission given before you can put that name into use.

> [ ] Step 95 - Eliminate any names in your list that would imply that you offer a professional service that you do not have the legal authority to offer.

Check Web Availability

Once you have a name, or preferably, a list of desired, permissible, names, you will want to check to make sure you can get the domain name for your company, or some variation if you so desire.

With everything moving online, it is arguably more important to be able to get the domain name than it is to get the trademark or secretary of state name reservation. The prime real estate online is the dot com. (".com") ending of your domain name (unless you have a specific reason for the other top level domain like .org for charities, or .me for a personal webpage or as a play on words).

To find out if your domain name is available, you need to go through a domain name registrar like GoDaddy.com. I use GoDaddy.com because it is very easy to use, but you can use any domain name register to search to see if the domain is available.

Tip: The company you're using will keep track of how often people search for names. If you search too often, or lots of other people have already searched, they may raise the price for the next time you visit.

For this searching part, you won't need a web expert because they've made this portion easy to use for anyone. Once you actually want to buy it, however, I'd recommend getting someone to help you unless you've been through this process before. You can't transfer a domain for several months after you buy it, so if your web designer wants to use it, they'll have to use your account, or have you redirect the nameservers to their hosting provider.

Tip: If you didn't understand, or aren't comfortable with, that last paragraph, hire someone to help buy it.

Additionally, if you get one of the instant websites that you can make with some web domain purchase companies, your site will look worse than it should and will contain a tacky advertisement for the company you bought it from. You don't want that.

A small investment here is incredibly worthwhile, as your website is often your company's first impression.

[ ] Step 96 - Check your list of names domain name availability and eliminate any that are not available in a variation that you are comfortable with.

Tip: .com is the most visited top level domain, .org is generally, but not required to be, used for nonprofits, and other top level domains are permissible, but are less commonly visited. If you can get the .com, you should, unless you are a nonprofit or have a specific reason for the other top level domain.

Check State Availability

Once you've found your name online, you also have to check with the secretary of state to ensure your name isn't taken. If it's free online, it's likely going to be free with the secretary of state because there are fifty states and hundreds of countries that could use the same domain and the secretary of state filing is only in your state.

Most states have a way to search existing registrations using the internet. If yours doesn't, you may have to call or write to the department in charge of company names and filings. Keep in mind that your name may still be rejected, even if it is available, if your state's office believes it to be in violation of any number of naming rules. In North Carolina, they list these rules in a guide on forming your company on the secretary of state's webpage. Most other states have similar guides.

[ ] Step 97 - Search your state's company records and eliminate any names that conflict with existing companies. Also, search after removing words such as "the," "a," and "and."

North Carolina Secretary of State's Corporation Search:
http://www.sosnc.gov/search/index/corp

Also keep in mind that even if your state approves the name and allows you to file, you may have an illegal name and may need to refile at a later date, or be subject to fines or a lawsuit if you're violating someone else's trademark or copyright.

Tip: If your name isn't currently taken, but was in the past
with a company that is now dissolved, you may have
troubles obtaining an EIN through the IRS. You may
either want to consider different names, or be prepared to
call their hotline and mail in a paper application.

Search Trademarks

Finally, you should run a search on the US Patent and Trademark Office (USPTO) to ensure that the name you're trying to use isn't trademarked. Since trademarks are separated into classifications, even if your name is trademarked, you should examine the trademark closely to see if it is trademarked in your classification. If it's not trademarked in your classification, you're good on this step. Otherwise, you don't want to use it because you may be violating someone else's trademark.

[ ] Step 98 - Search the USPTO.gov Trademark site to eliminate any names that violate others' trademarks.

USPTO Site: http://www.uspto.gov/

Registering the trademark with the USPTO gives you a registered trademark, and you should consider whether or not you should get your own trademark this way to protect your name from use by other people to steal your brand loyalty and goodwill.

There's another type of trademark, the common law trademark. This is the 'TM' symbol you see on a lot of trademarks. You can put the 'TM' on anything that qualifies as a trademark of your business. Anything, like your logo, that you use regularly in commerce can be trademarked this way unless it is trademarked by someone else, would likely create confusion with another company's trademark, or is excluded in any other way from being allowed to be trademarked.

[ ] Step 99 - Search your state trademark office to eliminate any name choices that conflict with someone's state registered trademark.

North Carolina State Trademark Search:
https://www.secretary.state.nc.us/trademrk/search.aspx

The word or slogan must also qualify as able to be trademarked. This analysis will come later on in this book. If it's close, you should do extensive research or seek out a trademark attorney.

[ ] Step 100 -   Once again, use Google or your favorite search engine to search for your trademark and arrangement of parts for your name. If there are any similar names in your industry in your geographic area, you should eliminate those names as well because they might have a common law trademark.

Every state has their own requirements for names. Yours may have specific requirements that are otherwise unaddressed in this book.

[ ] Step 101 -   Check with your state to see if there are any other requirements in choosing a name that you should be aware of and fulfill these requirements.

Choice of Entity

So, you've got a name and a business idea? You've done the hardest work. Everything else is a step by step process by comparison. If you're a creative type, you're about to get bored. Everything else to begin the company is fairly standardized. There is room for creativity, but not too much. If you get too carried away, you'll end up hurting yourself because, in the legal world, people like predictability and standardization.

The next step in this process is about determining which type of legal entity works best for you. As discussed before, the lack of a separate legal entity is called a sole proprietorship if owned individually and a general partnership if owned by two or more people. These options are full of risk because you maintain personal liability for every debt and liability of the company. Some people choose this route and just get enormous insurance policies. That's a valid way of doing things, but it doesn't have the protection for issues that exceed your insurance policy, nor does it protect against costs within your deductible.

Furthermore, once your company is making more or has more reach, you're losing a lot of money by maintaining the insurance policies you need when you could protect yourself equally by maintaining a smaller insurance policy and forming a separate entity to separate the legal liability from you personally. You should absolutely still maintain insurance because you're not going to close down your business for every medium or large cost. The protection is for the catastrophes and to prevent people from suing you personally in the first place.

Warning: This analysis can be very in depth for some companies and this book only provides a brief overview.

The next level, in terms of formality, is the limited liability company. This is frequently touted as the best choice for small business owners, and in many cases, that's going to be correct. An LLC is an incredibly versatile type of company. It can be taxed as a partnership, disregarded entity, or Subchapter C or S Corporation as needed. It has the ability to allocate profit and loss differently than you can allocate ownership. There are more relaxed formalities that need to be followed as well. You're able to have as many owners as you want and your owners can be any type of entity.

So, why wouldn't the LLC be a good choice? There are a lot of specific tax code benefits for stock transfers and acquisitions that affect corporations and not limited liability companies as well as employee stock options and benefits provided to owners. There are also weird legal effects of being an owner of an LLC versus an owner of a corporation because of the separate legal entity status of a corporation and the stocks instead of an ownership interest. LLCs are harder to set limitations on ownership than a corporation. If these reasons make an LLC the wrong choice for your situation, you may want to consider a Corporation.

The Subchapter C Corporation (C Corp) is the traditional corporation model. This model contains the 'double taxation' that you hear about with corporations. This means that it is taxed at the corporate level as well as if the profits are distributed out as dividends because dividend distributions are not allowed to be excluded from the corporate income. This double taxation can easily be avoided in smaller C Corps because salary is deductible from the corporate income for taxation purposes. C Corps are also advantageous because they're the prima facie investor vehicle due to the ease in which you can invest, transfer ownership, and avoid owner taxation until actually paid. C Corporations can also offer significantly more benefits to the owner than any other type of entity.

Investments in an LLC would result in a lot of additional work throughout the investment and sometimes taxation without earnings; therefore, a lot of higher level investors want to only invest in C Corps to limit the transaction and taxation cost of their investments. This isn't always the case, and the LLC can be structured in a way to make your investors happy. The necessary restructuring, however, increases your costs to set up.

Tip: Want to avoid the double taxation, spend down your accounts on business expenses or salary before the end of your fiscal year.

Despite all the tax code sections and other various differences, the final decision, in main street style companies, usually comes down to personal preference. Some people love the corporate structure and others love the free reign of the LLC. Most everything else is similar or convertible when it comes to your business. When in doubt, the LLC is a good starting point. You then want to find specific reasons why you wouldn't want an LLC or a specific reason you would want one of the other types of entities.

A lot of community colleges and universities will have seminars or clinics that will help you with choosing type of entity, and if those don't help or you want stronger advice, you can discuss this with your lawyer and CPA.

The nonprofit is also a valid choice among many new startups, but you need to make sure this is the one you want. The largest drawbacks of a nonprofit are that you cannot sell it, and you cannot receive income from it as a distribution. You may only receive salary and you do not own a nonprofit. The major benefits are that it has very strong liability protection and has a connotation about them that people trust.

You may also receive tax benefits if your state has specific tax benefits or if you file for a 501(c)(3) or similar tax treatment. These are complicated designations and take a very long time to get approved, so the cost of forming a 501(c)(3) is much higher than a corporation or LLC.

The following chart illustrates some areas where it is almost always more beneficial to go with one type over the other. The first column is a brief description of the nature of the business or a type of transaction, and the second column is typically the best choice.

Obviously, you can end up in more than one of these categories. For those situations, talk to your attorney.

Buying & Selling of Real Estate	LLC
Third Party Investors	Corp
Pass through Income (royalties, licenses, rent)	LLC
IPOs	Corp
Employee Stock Options	Corp
Profits and losses in custom proportions	LLC
Better owner benefits and stock codes	Corp
Receive donations	Nonprofit

[ ] Step 102 -   Choose which type of entity you want between LLC, Corporation, and Nonprofit.

S Corporations

The subchapter S Corporation is an election made through the IRS to obtain a unique hybrid taxation. As it is not a separate type of legal entity, becoming an S Corp requires that you are already either an LLC or Corporation. You must file a form 2553 with the IRS to become recognized as an S Corp for taxation purposes.

Tip: Form 2553 is a very easy form to complete. You likely will not need professional help to complete it and fax it.

The advantage to having an S Corp is that you might end up paying significantly less in employment taxes. You must first pay yourself a reasonable salary that is taxed as an employee's income, including the FICA taxes. After that, you pay yourself a distribution on equity, prorated to your equity interest in the company, and pay a much lower tax on all income above that determined "reasonable salary."

The primary disadvantages to having an S Corp are the limitations on ownership and how it makes certain deductions unavailable. In order to qualify to be taxed as an S Corp, you must have fewer than 100 owners, be owned completely by natural persons who are United States citizens, and your allocations of profits and losses after the salary must be in proportion to ownership interest. This means you cannot have any LLCs or corporations as owners.

S Corps have many requirements in order to stay an S Corp. Violation of any of these requirements, whether your fault or not, can result in conversion to C Corp status. Some of these requirements include the limitation to 100 shareholders, one class of shares, allocation of profit and loss in relation to ownership of stocks, only allowed to have real people as shareholders and the shareholders must be United States citizens. Any violation of these, even inadvertently, would result in loss of S Corporation status.

Tip: The IRS fax machine is regularly busy. Make the election early, and be prepared to try again.

Imagine the scenario where one of your partners decides to gift his ownership in the company to his son's LLC. This would automatically defeat the S Corporation election, so it is important, if you make this election, that your bylaws and shareholder agreements or operating agreement specify how and when ownership may be transferred both voluntarily and through death, bankruptcy, receivership, liens, and other involuntary or operation of law methods of transfer.

[ ] Step 103 -   Decide if the S Corporation tax election makes sense for your business or speak with your CPA to help decide this. If it does, we will come back to this a little later.

Sample Articles in North Carolina

To form your company, you will need to file the 'Articles' with the entity tasked with forming companies in your state. In North Carolina, this is the Department of the Secretary of State. As each state is a little different, we can only provide sample articles for the state of North Carolina. For other states, it is likely that your secretary of state's (or whichever entity handles formations in your state) webpage will have samples and even a guide on how to fill them out.

A list of resources, such as these forms, can be found on this book's website: www.checkmarkstartup.com/resources/.

LLC

For your LLC, there are a few required terms for your company's Articles of Organization. The most common parts are:

- Name of the Company. You name must include "LLC," "Limited Liability Company," or any other common abbreviation for a Limited Liability Company.
- Registered Agent and Address. This isn't required in all states, but it is the person or entity that is located within the state borders that is responsible for accepting service of process on behalf of the company. This is important because this is the place a person can sue a business in the event the business has wronged that person. Just by serving this person, even if the business owner never gets the lawsuit, subjects the business to the jurisdiction of the court.
- Principal Office Location. This also isn't required in all states, and isn't required in North Carolina, but it provides a backup for the registered agent in case service cannot be

obtained on the registered agent. It also provides the public with more information about your company.

Tip: If the Registered Agent misses a lawsuit, there is a chance your company may be dissolved. The Principal Office location is a second layer of defense against this.

- <u>Member Managed versus Manager Managed</u>. This is becoming less common and has been removed from North Carolina's articles. What this establishes is whether the Members (owners in an LLC) can make management decisions simply because they're Members, or whether Members must vote for a Manager or multiple Managers of the company. In NC, all Members are Managers automatically unless the Articles or Operating Agreement specify otherwise.
- <u>Organizer</u>. The Organizer does not necessarily have to be a Member, but the Organizer is the person who is setting up the LLC. This person has only the authority to set up the LLC, unless the Articles or Operating Agreement specify that she is a Member or Manager.

C Corp

Corporation Articles (Articles of Incorporation) contain a lot more information because of the nature of how corporations work. Each state has their own requirements of what has to be in the Articles of Incorporation, primarily company name, address, registered agent name, registered agent address, incorporator name and address, number of shares issued, types of shares issued, date started, and a signature of the incorporator.

The major difference between an LLC and a Corporation is the shares provisions.

- Number of Shares
- Classes of Shares

Since the articles are publicly accessible, it may be wise to include more in yours, if you're seeking investment. The more information in the articles, the more transparent your company will be. Many times, it may be a good idea to include a purpose section in the articles for investors.

You may want to keep certain other provisions, including purpose, more private by only including in the bylaws. How meetings are conducted isn't information the public needs to know because the public isn't invited to those meetings. Therefore, that kind of information should not be included in these Articles.

Keep in mind that if you're a charity, you will still have to submit your bylaws to the IRS, and they will be public record.

Partnership

A Partnership requires no filing to be effective. A partnership is formed when two people decide to go into business together and take any substantial step toward yielding a profit. This can include researching a location for their new company, creating a business plan, raising capital and more. Partnerships are easily formed because of how easy and quickly they are formed, it is important to be clear when discussing business ideas with people that you are not creating a partnership, just discussing.

Partnerships are also destroyed immediately when one partner leaves under most states' laws.

LP

Limited Partnerships are a specialized form of Partnership that incorporates limited liability with the functionality of a partnership. The main requirement is that there be at least one general partner (full liability) and that any limited partners have absolutely no control over the company. This type of entity is commonly used in real estate investing and other forms of investing or asset protection, and it shouldn't be used unless you have a compelling reason to do so.

LLP

Limited Liability Partnerships are also specialized structures.

Their uses also vary wildly between states.

The objective of the LLP is to operate like a general partnership but eliminate all or some of the personal liability on each partner for the actions of the other partners. Each partner would still be liable for his or her own actions, and in some states, the limitation of liability is only limited to certain causes of action, like contractual or negligence.

Some states even have limitations on who can use an LLP. In these states, only professionals like doctors, lawyers and architects can use the LLP; however, you will also find them being able to create professional corporations and professional LLCs.

You should have a compelling reason for choosing your organization type if you're not choosing an LLC, Corporation or nonprofit. These other types are highly specialized and can have extreme tax and liability consequences if chosen.

L3C

The L3C or LLLC (Low Profit Limited Liability Company) is a hybrid vehicle between nonprofits and limited liability companies. The only thing you really need to know about this is that it makes investing by private foundations when investing into a project based for-profit company that has charitable causes. Typically, foundations can only invest into non-profits, but this helps with the IRS compliance to ensure the funds are properly used.

If you're creating a company with a socially beneficial purpose that also may rely on foundation grants or funding, then consider doing some research into the L3C. Otherwise, you will not need to worry about this type of entity. Most states do not have this type of entity, so it may not even apply to you.

Nonprofit Corp

You wouldn't think so, but many times, the nonprofit is actually the type of entity you want. Most people assume you cannot make any money with a nonprofit, but that is not true. As a nonprofit, you're still allowed to pay yourself a salary. States have their own rules and, if you're attempting to become a charity, you'll have to abide by the IRS rules for charities as well.

To qualify as a nonprofit, none of the income of the company can be distributed to the owners as distributions. With for-profit companies, the excess income can be distributed to the equity owners. The most recognizable form of this is the corporate dividend. Nonprofit companies cannot have dividend type distributions, but there's nothing against a reasonable salary.

For example: If your nonprofit earns $80,000 per year, you can pay yourself a salary of $80,000 per year and end up with a net $0 in the nonprofit. In a typical for-profit company, you might retain some of that money in the company or invest in it because you can sell your portion of the company at a later date. Or, you might be able to pay yourself $60,000 and give a distribution or dividend of $20,000, if the tax reasons exist to do so. Nonprofits have no retained value in your ownership interest, nor do they allow for distributions. LLC owners are taxed on the income as soon as it is earned by the company and corporations pay corporate tax on excess income held by the company. The nonprofit alone can hold onto large sums of money without any income tax consequences.

This nonprofit structure is typically not the structure of choice, but it does make a lot of sense in socially beneficial companies or companies that are not looking to provide ownership value or distributions. There was one company that started with the purpose of bringing together a group of professionals to teach small businesses. After debating for a very long time, they agreed that nonprofit was the entity of choice for them because no one was going to earn any value on their ownership interest. They would just hold a board position.

Although there are some protections you can put in place, a nonprofit is a risky move because you don't necessarily get to 'own' the company. Instead, you will have a board of directors. Some states do not require a minimum number of board members. In those states, you can have 1 board member (yourself), but you still won't be able to pass this company on to your children or your family. If you're in a state that requires higher numbers of board members, you will run the risk of being voted out of the company. The IRS also has some strict requirements for number of board members and the relationships these board members may have with each other should you choose to obtain charity status.

Tip: If you don't know which type of company structure would be best for you and your company, talk to your attorney, and she will be able to help you.

Governing Document Agreements

No matter what type of company you choose, you will need to set up at an agreement with yourself and the other members of your company. Each type of company has its own type of agreement, outlined below.

Even if you're alone in the company, you should set up something. Why? When we make agreements with ourselves and write it down, we have a far greater chance of following through.

In this agreement, we're outlining the way the company runs. The agreement is an overview of the values and operations of the company. Having clear values and operations laid out in the beginning is important for consistency. It's also important to think about these things before you start the company. Giving a fair amount of thought to these ideas before even starting will accelerate your business beyond where the typical company starts.

Bylaws

Bylaws are the corporate guidelines for a corporation type company. This can be either a subchapter S or subchapter C corporation.

[ ] Step 104 -   If you're not forming a corporation, or nonprofit, skip ahead to the Operating Agreement section.

The bylaws contain different information based on the different company. It is strongly recommended that you include a purpose, values and mission statement in the bylaws so you always keep true to the core values that you've established earlier.

[ ] Step 105 -   Using our template, fill in the General Provisions portion of your bylaws, including the name, office location, registered agent, and any other general provisions your template requests.

As an officer or director, you're obligated to keep to your bylaws. However, as a shareholder, you're able to change them or waive enforcement of the bylaws. The rules you set in the bylaws are the rules your directors and officers are required to follow, as well as some rules for your shareholders.

When you're a sole owner in a corporation, you wear many hats. You will be the shareholder, the director, and CEO. In each of these roles, you will have different rules to follow and it is very important to keep them separated in any documentation.

Hint: Corporate formalities must be followed to maintain corporate status and liability protection. One of these formalities is the requirement to have directors separate from shareholders. In each of these roles, you're required to operate as the hat you're wearing. You cannot act as a shareholder and a director at the same time.

Part of the corporate structure is the separation of ownership and management. Owners are shareholders, but they delegate the management of their company to the board of directors, also called the managers.

The bylaws will also contain information on how the board of directors operates, which committees can be formed and what they're able to do and what officers the corporation will have. Bylaws will typically outline how meetings will work and how conflicts of interest will be handled.

> [ ] Step 106 - In Article 2 of your bylaws, list what powers the board of directors has, how they're voted into office, how many directors you have, how they can be removed from office, a conflict of interest policy, and any qualifications your directors may have.

Tip: We've provided most of these terms for you in our template at www.checkmarkstartup.com/resources.

Directors appoint the President, CEO, Executive Director, or other officers of the Corporation.

> [ ] Step 107 - In Article 3 of your bylaws, list what officer positions there are, what powers those officers have, how they're appointed, and any other terms that limit their authority.

It is also recommended to include a provision on how to amend the bylaws. There may be default rules in your state, but setting a clear policy is advisable to avoid any issue later on.

> [ ] Step 108 - In Article 4 of your bylaws, outline how the bylaws can be changed, how disputes are settled, and a provision that states how these bylaws were ratified, with signatures underneath.

Bylaws can contain provisions on any type of rules your company will have, but typically, the bylaws are restricted to the operations of shareholders, directors and officers. Anything beyond that can be made by board resolution or by a decision of the officers.

*Example: Dress code shouldn't appear in the bylaws.
Instead, you'd place your dress code in an employee
handbook or some company policy drafted by the board,
CEO, or other corporate officers.*

[ ] Step 109 -   Go through the remainder of the sample
Bylaws and make any changes you see fit, but be careful
not to make drastic changes or get too creative.

Before your Bylaws can be effective, you must have your initial meeting of the shareholders. To do this, you have to have all the initial shareholders present to ratify the bylaws. Ratification requires unanimous consent, but in the future, any changes can be made pursuant to the percent you choose in the bylaws.

You must also appoint your initial board during the initial meeting of the shareholders. Boards can consist of as many people as you want. In some states, there are requirements for numbers, and 501(c)(3) organizations require at least three nonrelated board members.

*Tip: For nonprofits, your initial meeting of the
shareholders is actually called an initial meeting of the
directors (or members if a member-based nonprofit).*

[ ] Step 110 -   Hold your initial meeting of the
shareholders, ratify the bylaws, and sign the shareholder
ratification. During this meeting vote in your initial
directors and appoint your officers, as you defined them in
the bylaws.

We've provided you with sample ratification and appointment documents at the end of your bylaws. Use these or modify them as needed.

Operating Agreement

An operating agreement is the limited liability company version of the bylaws. It contains very similar provisions; however, because it applies to the members of a limited liability company instead of the company itself, the operation is quite different.

Operating agreements and partnership agreements are very similar in nature. The operating agreement contains items that the members agree to when it comes to how they will run the company between the members. Each member will need to sign the initial operating agreement, whereas the bylaws only needs enough votes from directors and shareholders to enact.

In a limited liability company, the members are the owners. In a corporation, the owners are shareholders. This creates a difference in operation since the shareholders are typically not bound by the bylaws simply because they're shareholders. Members of an LLC, on the other hand, are bound by the operating agreement.

[ ] Step 111 -   Using our template, fill in Article I, General Provisions with the name and other basic information about your company.

Because this agreement is the sole determination for how members operate together in a company, it should be incredibly detailed. The less ambiguity there is in this document, the less likely there will be harmful disagreement down the road.

[ ] Step 112 -   In Article II, choose one of the options for the Additional Capital that you want for your company and delete the others.

A large number of entrepreneurs that get together to form a company believe that they do not need an operating agreement, stating things like "we're best friends (or family), there's no way we would have a problem" and "we don't have time to form an agreement like that." These entrepreneurs are looking for trouble.

The "best friends/family" approach is troublesome because your relationship with the person is personal, meaning any disagreement (and there will be many) has a greater chance of being taken personally. You actually have a greater chance of having a falling out if you are best friends than you do if you're business acquaintances.

Since you're best friends/family, you'll want to put anything business related down in writing ahead of time. This will allow you to be best friends/family after anything goes sour. It is, however, more important to understand the agreement than it is to just have it written down.

[ ] Step 113 -   For Distributions (Article III), you can't change the order of those items we've provided much, but you can add other things after the Company Debts.

Tip: Some people like to put specific loans or commissions within the distributions.

[ ] Step 114 -   Read through Article V, the Management Section, and make any changes to the way the management is laid out, as well as fill in any names of management you want.

Tip: K.I.S.S. Keep it simple ...silly. The more clever you think your management, or other, provisions are, the more likely they will have loopholes, ambiguities, or issues in their interpretation. This principle applies even to the most seasoned attorneys and entrepreneurs.

The complaint that there isn't enough time is a terrible argument. Putting expectations and operations down in writing actually saves a company a significant amount of time. This eliminates any hesitation between giving orders or handling disputes. The inefficiencies in operations are lessened when you have a clear operating agreement in place.

Since this is an agreement between members, it is important to include things such as how much time and money each member is required to contribute, and in doing so, how much equity does that member get. Are there any strings attached to the member's equity? If so, they'd be in this agreement. Strings can include vesting schedules, buyback provisions, right of first refusal, forfeiture clauses, and more.

Tip: If you want to include any of these strings attached to ownership like vesting schedules, right of first refusal or forfeiture clauses, you should contact an attorney to help because these areas can really affect your rights as an owner as well as impact your company's standing with your state or the SEC.

You will also include what happens when a member leaves in your operating agreement because members leave, and you won't want to be stuck not knowing how to carry on the business. Furthermore, you may not want the heirs of that person to be in charge once he passes away. This is actually very important to include, even if the desired result is a winding down of the business. This provision is vital to have in order to enjoy a peaceful transition between members.

Along the same lines, you will want to include a set of rules for how a new member can join and what that process would look like. This includes how to determine how much equity she will receive, who decides whether or not she may join the company and what she would be responsible to do. Since limited liability companies can allocate profits and losses in any way, you will want to include a provision that describes how new members would be included in this analysis if it isn't distributed in proportion with equity.

[ ] Step 115 - In Article VI, fill in the blanks left for you in our template.

Members' rights should also be included. You will want to know what kinds of decisions the members can make and what rights they have as members opposed to the rights of managers. In the same section, you will want to define the members' responsibilities. If one member is responsible for all the labor and another is in charge of financing, that's important to make clear before the business starts. Otherwise, unclear expectations will lead to ambiguous functioning as a company.

[ ] Step 116 -   In Article VII, Transfers, read through, but leave this part be unless you speak with a professional. Certain transfers can violate SEC law, and certain limitations on transfers are not permitted. What we have is a fairly safe version for you. Also, leave Article VIII as is.

[ ] Step 117 -   For Article IX, fill in the blanks and delete any Events of Dissociation that will not apply to your circumstances.

The operational details must also not be overlooked. Any specific operational plans should be outlined in the operating agreement as well as how records are kept, how banking is done and any other company wide administrative requirements.

[ ] Step 118 -   Go back through the Operating Agreement and modify any operational details you want to adjust.

Finally, it's important to include provisions on how to settle disputes amongst the members. Absent clear rules on this, members may be inclined to take things up in litigation when there is a dispute instead of settling in negotiations; other members may feel helpless and shy away from the company altogether. Having clearer dispute resolution policies in place will provide for more streamlined resolutions.

[ ] Step 119 -   For Article XII, fill in the blanks we've left for you.

[ ] Step 120 - In Exhibit A, fill in the names, addresses, and ownership percentage of each Member as well as any cash contribution or labor requirements of the Members.

Operating Agreements are not valid unless signed by all of the Members. After the first Operating Agreement is made, you can specify how changes are to be made in the future. Some states have different rules on how to modify or ratify an Operating Agreement, so if you're looking to ratify by less than unanimous consent, you should check with your state laws or your attorney.

[ ] Step 121 - Now that you've got a valid, binding, and clear Operating Agreement, print it, have all owners review and sign it, date it, and store the original(s) in a safe spot.

Tip: Scanning your operating agreement is a great way to store it. Also, you can make copies or separate originals for each owner.

Partnership Agreement

A partnership agreement is very similar to an operating agreement. Each state has different default rules for partnerships and limited liability companies, but it's a much better idea to fully define your expectations in these agreements. That way, you don't rely on changing rules or ambiguous expectations when trying to determine how the company is intended to run or how to resolve a dispute between owners.

Business Licenses

You may be required to get a business license to operate your business. Licenses vary through different states, counties within states, cities and even different industries or products. One of the most common business licenses is the general business license. It is called different things in different places, but it gives you the right to conduct business in that region for a specific period of time. Sometimes, this license is referred to as a business privilege license because it gives you the privilege of conducting business in that area.

When you sell certain products, like alcohol, you may need additional licenses because the product is regulated.

[ ] Step 122 -   Check with your state to see what licenses
you need.

Tip: In NC, to see what licenses you're required to have, you can call the free hotline: 919-447-7828.

CHAPTER 14 - BUILDING THE TEAM

No one can do everything in a business and those that try end up getting virtually nothing done. Think about the vast amount of things you need to do each day in your business. Are you incredibly efficient at each and every skill your company needs? If you answered yes, you're lying to yourself.

Using a bank is outsourcing a portion of your business. Banks will offer far more than just storage of your company's funds. They accept checks, cash them into your account, transfer money on your behalf when you write checks, offer payroll, merchant services and much more.

You typically do not find a business owner who can do the marketing, business development, product development and administration of the business efficiently. That's why it is important to build a team. Not everyone on the team needs to be an owner of the business. Outsourcing to independent contractors or hiring employees are equally viable options. The difference is that independent contractors and employees need to be paid out of cash flow whereas co-owners can be paid in equity and future earnings.

Michael Jordan was arguably the best basketball player of all time. He fine-tuned his skills at basketball and it showed. When he switched to baseball, he was well below average, even though they require similar skills. Similarly, an amazing salesperson should make sales and a great accountant should stick to accounting.

But what about cash flow? I know, unless you're an incredibly well funded startup, it is impossible to immediately hire a team of specialists to come in and take care of everything you need in your company. Believe me, I've been there. You need to prioritize, and you do that by analyzing the time you spend and the money you spend each day. If you find out you're losing a lot of time doing your bookkeeping, that might be the first task to outsource. If you spend your day driving, consider hiring a salesperson or a driver. This process of analyzing your return on time and money investment is one of the most important in your business and will be vital in other areas beyond outsourcing needs.

Furthermore, if you do not have the cash flow to hire someone, yet know you need their services to make those hours available, consider entering into a barter or partnership arrangement. If you offer a service that this person needs, you can trade based on hours or billable rates. If, however, they don't want your service or you don't want theirs, you can offer equity in your company or some measure of profit from future cash flows.

There are creative ways to enter into these working relationships; however, they're harder to come by because everyone must worry about their cash flow, just like you are. They also require your business partner to have faith in the quality of your work and the value of your services.

Legal Tip: Barter arrangements must be reported as taxable income even though no money is changing hands. The measure is "anything of value" in exchange for your goods or services.

Identify Your Own Skills

The first step in building a team is identifying the skills where you excel. For most business owners, the primary skill is the one thing the business does. Attorneys are typically good at practicing law. Web developers are good at programming computers. You may even have some secondary skills where you are proficient. I have a colleague who makes websites and does bookkeeping. He is exceptional at both of these areas, but he is not very good at marketing or business development.

You do this step just like you would the values. Write down every skill you have. You should start by listing the classifications of Production, Expansion, Protection and Administration. Then, you want to get more specific into categories. In expansion, you may have topics like marketing, branding, networking and more. Your production categories are likely going to be your more populated category. Protection is typically scarce for most business owners unless you're in a legal, insurance, or strategic planning business. Administration depends on the person, but would include skills such as bookkeeping, record keeping, scheduling and more.

[ ] Step 123 - Make a list of your proficient skills. Focus primarily on those things that you use, or would use, in your company.

A sample list for Bobby, a software developer, is located in Appendix IV.

[ ] Step 124 - If you have more than one founder, make a separate list for each founder. We'll be using them in a short while.

Identify the Skills Needed

Every company has a list of skills necessary to make that company a success. The larger the company, the more unmanageable this is. With us smaller companies, we can pretty easily plan out exactly what we're looking for by outlining what is necessary in the four areas of a business: Production, Expansion, Protection, and Administrative.

[ ] Step 125 - The next step is to identify and list the skills your company needs. You do this in the exact same way you would for yourself using the best affordable position your company would be in and with your goal, mission statement and branding values in mind.

> *The same client, Bobby, listed the skills his company needs in Appendix IV.*

Though Bobby's list could be more thorough, this is a good illustration of the kinds of things he has to think about. To fulfill these, you either need to hire someone to do them or contract out the service. Holes in your needed services typically result in inefficient management of your company. If at all possible, ensure that each of the areas you write down are covered by someone in your company or outsourced to someone you can trust.

Keep in mind that if there's a gap, you're likely going to have to fill it yourself. Determine if that's something you're willing to do and how much it takes away from your other areas.

Tip: Using a spreadsheet is a good way to see all of the skills and people fulfilling them. The first column

	A	B	C
1	**Skills**	**Richard**	**Eric**
2	Case Law Research	90	50
3	Brief Writing	60	70
4	Litigation Drafting	60	90
5	Trial Appearances	20	85
6	Equity Drafting	80	25
7	Contract Drafting	95	75

would be the skills and then the following columns would be the individual proficiencies in this skills. A 0 would be none at all.

Identify What You're Willing to Give Up

Nobody works for free. That's the way things work. People do, however, work for things other than cash. Frequently, you will find people will work for ownership in part of the company, trade for services, or in exchange for goodwill and marketing on their behalf.

You will always have to give up something to get someone else to work for you. You must decide before you engage with someone what you are willing to give up. Keep in mind that the more flexible you are with what you're willing to give up, the less time you will spend searching for and negotiating with a person to fulfill these needs because you will have a wider pool of people to search from.

Tip: You can continue to use this same analysis as you begin to grow. You'll identify what new skills are required, and what areas you want to start removing from certain workers.

Salary

You've already done the cash flow analysis at this point, so you know what money you have available to be able to pay someone. If you have the cash flow and believe it would be best spent on this service or service provider, then salary is likely the best opportunity. You can hire people part-time as well.

Keep in mind skills can be combined into one position, so no one skill is usually a fulltime salary.

Outsourced individuals are usually cheaper because you do not have to worry about access to your entire company, sick days, vacation days, FICA withholding, insurances, etc. If you already have these systems set up and you're going to fully utilize the employee, hiring an employee may be better. It's a case-by-case analysis when determining whether or not to hire a person as an employee or an independent contractor.

If, however, you want to hire someone as an independent contractor, you will need to make sure that you've actually hired an independent contractor. More on this analysis will come later on in this book because it is important to make sure it is done right or the Department of Labor and the IRS will be knocking at your door with large fines and penalties.

---

*Tip: The IRS and usually state Departments of Labor
have resources to help determine if a position should be
classified as an employee or independent contract.*

Equity

Equity is another option for compensation. Especially in tech startups, this seems to be a big deal. There are many developers, entrepreneurially-minded individuals, and service providers who are interested in owning a chunk of your next big idea.

This area is a little more complex because there's risk management involved. In order to determine a fair amount of equity to give up, you have to determine both what your company is worth and what the service is worth to your company.

Valuation is going to be a major source of contention in this negotiation. Since you believe your company will be extremely successful, you're going to have a higher valuation than someone who is not as close to it as you. This is part of the reason why you will want someone who believes in the idea as much as you. (The other reason is they are more committed to doing a good job.)

Once you generate the valuation of both, you must create the agreement and terms to pass that equity to your new partner. We will explore all the interesting facets of equity agreements and team agreements later on in this book. It is much harder to get rid of an equity holder than it is an employee or contractor, so there needs to be significantly more vetting up front.

Combination of Both

Sometimes your provider is going to want some security and some upside benefit in case the idea succeeds. In these cases, you can provide some cash as well as some equity or stock options. These transactions are very common in larger corporate companies. The "employee stock option pool" is one name for the discretionary stocks that the CEO or management of the company can issue to employees as encouragement to do a good job.

In your case, it's done to preserve cash flow, provide the

incentive and keep most of the equity that you'd like to maintain in order to hold onto the majority share of your company.

Legal Tip: There are many rules when it comes to compensation, especially if the compensation is below minimum wage. Before setting up one of these combination plans, you should speak with an attorney. Doing this wrong could put you in trouble with the IRS or Department of Labor.

Barter for Services

If you're a professional service provider or similar, you may have the option to barter services with other professional service providers. Although you must still report any value earned from your work on your tax forms, this is still incredibly beneficial because you preserve your all-important cash flow. Bookkeepers, lawyers, CPAs, realtors, business coaches, virtual secretaries, marketers, print companies, and similar providers are valuable service providers that are needed by other businesses. Therefore, these are perfect candidates for barter for service arrangements if they're also willing to enter into that relationship.

It's important to keep in mind that you should only set these arrangements up with service providers that you trust. It would do you no good to have credit built up in someone else's business if you do not want to use it. Furthermore, you wouldn't use that credit to handle any of your clients' work because once again, you don't trust them.

These arrangements are set up in all sorts of ways and are dependent on the two people to determine which is best. Some common ways are to just bill normally and reserve the credit until fully paid back, trade one specific item for another ahead of time or just have an ongoing "I'll help you" relationship. This last one is least advisable because it's too open-ended. You should have some limitations and terms defined so that there's no confusion as to the extent and scope of the relationship.

Since two different service providers typically have different prices, it's important to understand exactly how much each person's time is worth. A bookkeeper may end up doing four hours of work for every one hour an attorney does in one of these relationships. As long as both parties are fine with it, there's no problem. There may be problems if the parties didn't discuss this ahead of time and one party anticipates exchanging one hour for one hour of time. The attorney wouldn't think this is fair because her time is billed at a greater rate than the bookkeeper.

Marketing/Publicity

It's common for companies to take on work for free, but in exchange that company gets a certain level of publicity out of the arrangement. You see this most commonly with charities and early stage startup companies that have no money.

Companies want to good press from doing quality work for good causes. These aren't guaranteed, nor should they be expected, but it's an option. Keep in mind that if you are the charity or nonprofit looking for this arrangement, you will get rejected many times before you find the services, if you ever do. The time you spend looking for the free work may be better spent fundraising to hire a service provider instead. This is a consideration you should keep in mind.

There may be strings attached, like sponsorship notations on advertisements or coauthoring press releases. These strings may be a small price to pay, but keep in mind it's still a price and may take away from your brand or require a significant amount of your time.

A lot of the companies that do these types of arrangements are doing so because their brand is already hurt from some bad publicity. You'd be associated with that bad publicity, at least in part, because you're working with these companies. When you pay for the service, you don't have to worry as much about linking yourself to bad publicity because they typically won't be doing this for the publicity connection. You can also negotiate confidentiality for the relationship.

Completing the Analysis

[ ] Step 126 -   For each of the blank spots on your skills needed analysis, write down how much time it will likely take and how much you're willing to give up for each item. You can have multiple options for each as well.

Find the Team

You now know which skills you need and what you're willing to give up, but how do you find and interview the right people? Fortunately, you already have the tools in place to know how to vet the potential team members. Using what we've put together, you'll be checking to be sure that your hire falls under the amount you can give up, that she has the necessary skills, and that she shares most or all of the desired company values.

You have to trust the potential candidate. In any business transaction, trust is the most important aspect. You have to believe that this person is going to do the best job possible for you and have to trust that this candidate will maintain the values that are important to your company. Any deviation from that, especially early on, hurts your corporate culture and creates a sickness that customers and clients can sense.

There are many different ways to find these individuals from networking to paid searches, and everything in between.

Networking

Networking is one of the best ways to find quality people that fit your criteria, especially when you're looking for business-to-business service providers. All you have to do is let your trusted networking connections know what you're looking for and they'll be more than eager to make the introductions to their trusted service providers.

Networking is a fairly simple concept that gets butchered by so many. Networking, is about building relationships with a group of people who can mutually benefit from knowing each other. How you meet these people and how to best utilize these relationships is where the work lies.

Everyone does some form of networking. When you go to church, meet coworkers, have friends over for drinks, and any other time to interact with other people, you are networking. There are places where networking for business is the goal most people have, and we commonly refer to these at networking events. You can find networking events on event sites like Eventbrite and Meetup, and these are great starting places if you do not know where else to look.

My personal favorite place to look is by asking people I already know and trust. This is a good way to ensure you're only going to high quality events.

There are a few rules when it comes to networking that you should be aware of. These rules help ensure that you get the best long term return on your efforts.

First and foremost, you must approach this as a relationship building opportunity. When you attempt to sell directly at an event, you end up being "that guy," and you end up ruining whatever relationships you could have gotten.

Think of it this way: Would you rather get an attorney as a customer of yours, or many of that attorney's clients? The relationships you build will send you referrals overtime, so it yields more benefit and saves you future work.

Secondly, business events are for business purposes. If you meet someone new and you're overly friendly, you may leave that new connection with an uneasy feeling. I see this all the time at events where an older man gets friendly and sometimes handsy with women who are there networking. This is an absolute no, as it is not only a variety of illegal, immoral, and rude interactions (depending on what you're doing), it also destroys your personal brand.

Thirdly, be sure to nurture your relationships. You cannot meet someone once and expect that person to trust you enough to send referrals. It happens, but it is not that common. Instead, be sure to follow up and meet outside the event. If you can, and you think this person is a good referral source, you should meet regularly. Be sure to find ways to help your new connection as well.

Fourth, and definitely not final, remember that you are your personal brand. What you do at any point in public reflects on your company. Keep your values in mind as you're interacting with other people. If your values are strong personally, this is not a problem.

There are many other tips, suggestions, and rules on networking available on my personal website at www.bobholz.com.

[ ] Step 127 - For now, you need to identify those people you already trust, and ask for their introductions to people who fulfill these skills in a way that meets your values and the things you are willing to give up.

Tip: Be as clear as you can, but also be mindful of your connections' time, as they don't want to read a full employment description. Offer to provide greater details upon request.

Ask Advisors

If you have trusted advisors like an attorney, CPA, business coach, or other type of advisor, you can and should ask them for help finding the ideal candidate. They understand your business and have a professional network already, so they will hopefully be able to make introductions to the type of people you are looking for.

A caveat to this is to not put 100% faith in your advisors opinion. Your advisor is there to make recommendations, but you're the only person who will be able to tell if the candidate is truly a good fit for your company.

[ ] Step 128 - Reach out to your advisors exactly as you would your trusted networking connections.

Post Ads

The traditional way to find candidates is to post advertisements wherever it is suitable to do so. This could be at local universities, a newspaper, trade journals, craigslist, and recruitment websites. The good part about doing it this way is that you'll likely receive a wider variety of interest than you would have through the more pointed approaches; however, the benefit is also a hazard.

You need to determine how much time you have to go through applications, resumes, sample work product and whatever else you ask candidates to provide. On top of that, you will be conducting interviews and should send a letter to each applicant either rejecting or inviting them to join you. These things all take time, and time is a limited commodity.

A good note right now is that one of the benefits of being an entrepreneur is your ability to set your own hours. This shouldn't mean you'll be working fewer hours. Shorter work weeks are a goal, but if you take time off early and often, your company will not grow like it should. Each day you take off or work shorter hours is a day that you're leaving money on the table. Note that vacations and downtime are an investment in your mental energy, opposed to regularly working shorter days. There is a balance between taking time off to recharge versus taking time off to not work.

[ ] Step 129 -   If posting ads is a strategy you would like to employ, write the ad you will place, identify places you will be posting the ad, and submit the ad to be posted.

[ ] Step 130 -   If your ad posting strategy requires money, revisit your budget to either add this in or make sure that it fits in your budget.

Professional Recruiters

If you're hiring an employee or co-owner, professional recruiters can be a huge help. They cost a significant amount of money to hire, but a good recruiter is worth her weight in gold for the time and stress she saves you.

Typically, recruiters charge you a percentage of the first 1-2 years' salaries to find you the candidate you're looking for. You only owe this money if you hire a candidate they proposed and most of the time, they'll have you pay this fee over time.

[ ] Step 131 -   If recruiters are a strategy you would like to employ, figure out what recruiters work in needed field in your area and contact them to set up meetings.

Hackathons, Meetup, Entrepreneur Groups

Although it fits into the networking category, there's a specific subset of networking events that are geared toward building a team for your business. These events help pair up people with differing skills so that a stronger company can be formed. One of the favorites for this author is the Hackathon, an event where people have 24 hours to a weekend to create a company or product and prove its worth. It's a great place to meet other entrepreneurial-minded individuals on top of potentially creating a great company.

Local groups like the Chamber of Commerce will sometimes have events that are geared toward putting a team together as well.

[ ] Step 132 -   If this is an option you're interested in using, look up groups in your area and see if they have any of these types of events.

Do Not Settle

This happens all the time: you find an applicant you really like and trust, but she doesn't have all of the skills you need. Or you find someone who has all of the skills you need, but he doesn't have the values you need or seems untrustworthy.

It's important to not settle for less than you need. You especially do not want to give up the amount you were going to give up for the perfect candidate if you receive less than you were willing to bargain for.

If you cannot trust the person, there will be issues later on. Not only will it make you spend a lot of time and energy watching over their shoulder, but it's also part of the human psychology that if you are not trusted, you act untrustworthy. We gravitate toward how we are expected to act, most noticeably in a business sense. It's basically a self-fulfilling prophecy.

If the person is missing the skills you need for this position, you'll be getting less than you bargain for. Segmenting skills has not only a transaction cost by having to interview, manage, and hire more people, but it also comes with a premium per person. Specialization is a great tool running an efficient company; however, if a person is underworked, specialization will cost you.

It's also important to determine if you need two people. Overworking one person with two skills is worse than paying two people for two skills. If each person is working at less than 50% capacity, then, absent another good reason, it was unwise to segment the skills into two different people.

There are many other valid reasons to hire two people instead of one for the same skills. If you want the advice of the two people beyond just the skill set you had in mind, you're adding another skill to their job description: business development and advice. This could be beneficial or it may not.

The financial equation for determining if you should hire someone is simple. Is the rate of return equal or higher than other ways to spend the same amount of money? The difficulty is determining the variables. The cost is the net present value of the price you pay in salary, equity or otherwise combined with the time you will have to spend training them, working with them, insurances and any other variable costs that are new because this employee was hired.

The gain, on the other hand, is a prediction of the net present value of the increase in revenue and value of the company. There are complex equations and people who make a significant amount of money doing this analysis for you; however, if you hire the person to run this analysis, you'd be increasing the cost of hiring this team member and would therefore make it less likely you'd hire him.

To prevent this increased cost of hiring, your analysis winds up being an educated gut feeling that you rely on. You know your business better than anyone else, so you know what you need and what that person will bring to your team. In the course of your business, you'll likely make bad hires, but if you keep track of their work performance and the value they bring in, you'll be sure to only keep the good ones.

The analysis is far more difficult when looking at administration or protection, but you should either look to the prevention of loss as the ultimate gain or the free time you now have that you can spend doing more important things. These are important gains.

For example, if you hire an attorney to write your contracts for you, you will want to ensure that the net present value of the risk of something preventable going wrong in the contract multiplied by the potential loss under that contract is more than the cost of the attorney. For a lot of small business owners, it doesn't make sense to hire an attorney at certain stages in their business because the money doesn't make sense. For others, it doesn't make sense not to.

Author's Note: Yes, I'm a business attorney, so it should be more believable when I say you might not need an attorney. This isn't to say you'll be protected without one, but it means that the risk times the potential loss is less than the price of the attorney. You may still lose out under this analysis, but the math says your money should be invested elsewhere, unless you are a risk-adverse person.

The way you determine the value of a candidate is through the interview. In an interview, you want to determine only a few things.

First, is the candidate trustworthy and someone you could work with? You come to this conclusion through hypothetical situations, their references, and your gut feeling about him or her.

Second, does this candidate share the values of the company? You could ask the candidate what her values are, but a good candidate will already know the company's values and respond with those if she is aiming to get the position. A better way to determine a person's values is by asking questions that expose them. For example: if you want to know if the person values charity, you can ask questions about how she would plan a community service day or other policies you could enact to promote social good.

Third, you need to know how proficient the candidate is at the skills you're looking for her to fulfill. Past work product and competency questions are very useful for determining these areas.

Finally, you need to determine the value the candidate brings to the company. A lot of this analysis should be done by you ahead of time, but each candidate will be greater or less depending on their proficiency, work ethic, and other skills she brings to the table. A candidate's five or ten year plan is a good starting point to determine the long term success she will bring.

> [ ] Step 133 -   For each candidate, determine the ROI. For certain positions, we've included the formula below.

$$ROI = \frac{Anticipated\ Gains\ or\ Savings}{Cost\ of\ Hiring}$$

Anything above 1 is profitable, but that may not be your desired profit margin. Profit margins depend on your time, investment, industry, and many other things. The higher ROIs are the things you want to invest in.

> [ ] Step 134 -   For each candidate, reject him or her if you cannot answer yes to the following questions: (1) Is the ROI above your required profit margin? (2) Do they share the values of the company? (3) Do you believe they will be able to fulfill, with a high level of competency, the skills required in the position? (4) Do you trust the candidate?

Make the Offers

Once you find the candidate (or candidates) who has the values, the skills, and the trust you need, you will make the offer. Offers should always be in writing to protect you.

Legal Tip: Employment contracts can be as simple as an email stating how much the person will get paid, when he or she will start, what requirements there are of the job and how long the contract goes for.

Any key details should be spelled out in writing, not only for future reference, but to protect you in case things go awry. If your new hire is an employee, you will need a handbook and other policies put in place before he begins work. However, he may not be required to sign any contract (though it is highly recommended that he does) because his beginning to work is acceptance of the contract.

> [ ] Step 135 - If your hire is an employee, you can still send the offer letter, but include that it is contingent upon signing the employee handbook, employee contract, and whatever other human resources documents you need signed. We'll discuss these shortly.

The more you have to lose with an employee, the more formal the contract should be. If you want a non-competition agreement, a provision that does not allow assignment of the work, or other complicated provisions, you should certainly seek out legal advice, as these areas of law are changing constantly and are very different in each state.

Fortunately, if you don't yet want to build a relationship with an attorney, there are legal clinics that work with entrepreneurs at many law schools, incubators and bar associations. If you have access to these, they will give you legal advice on the specific questions you may have, but they cannot provide the level of experience a private practice attorney can provide. The services they provide vary, but you can at least get some level of guidance.

Your offer should also contain a reply-by date. This will give you some certainty of whether or not your candidate is actually interested. It's standard to give fourteen days' notice, but in faster-moving companies, you can give the requirement of far less. Some companies give 24 hours because they need to know immediately.

Once your offer is out there, you wait for an acceptance. This is a good time to reject all but your top five candidates. It's great for relationship building to send out a letter letting the applicants know that they haven't been selected, but you'll keep their resume on file in case anything comes up.

> [ ] Step 136 - Send professional rejection letters to the candidates who did not get selected.

[ ] Step 137 -   Once you receive the acceptance from your candidate, you then reject the other candidates. If your candidate rejects your offer, you can either negotiate or send the offer to the backup candidates.

Earlier, you listed the amount you were willing to give up, so don't go above that. You were clearer minded then than you are now. At this point, you are star-struck by a great candidate and unless she adds something else beyond the skills you were looking for, you should stick to your valuation.

Renegotiation can consist of restructuring the deal so you are still giving up the same value. Mix between equity and salary is a possibility if you're willing to part with both. Setting up incentive programs for cash if certain milestones are met is also a great way to incentivize people to join your company.

One of best ways to encourage people to join your company is to offer benefits. At the company level, many benefits are tax-deductible business expenses where, if provided by the employee, would be paid for by after-tax dollars. Therefore, you can provide $500 per month in benefits and the employee appears to be gaining an extra $550-$600 instead.

Health plans are the most common type of employee benefit you'll see, but the list is extensive. Even if your employee doesn't ask for specific benefits, it is likely a good idea to offer as many as you can afford because you can deduct all of (or a portion of) the expense from their wages, depending on how you structure the benefits. Most employee benefits count the same as ordinary business expenses, just as salary does.

Revisit Business Plan

Every time you bring in a new key employee or someone who influences the way the business is run, you will want to revisit the business plan. Of course, this should not be the only time you revisit the business plan. Revisitation should be as common as possible. If you're not visiting your business plan at least once a month, you're likely missing out on the efficiency aspect that the plan brings to your business.

Depending on her ability to influence the company, you may see a lot of new changes. If the new hire is a manager of a specific department, you should guide her through the process of listing her own values, the company values, the department values based on the company values, and then listing the mission statement and micro business plan a department would have.

If this team member does not have any ability to influence the company (which is unheard of in small companies), she should still have access to read through and learn from the business plan as it stands right now. Before showing her, make sure that you've updated it to reflect any changes that may have occurred since bringing in this new team member.

Legal Tip: If there are trade secrets or information that can harm you if used by another company, you should include a nondisclosure agreement in your employment agreements. In more advanced cases, you may also want a non-competition agreement to protect you.

The most likely scenario is that you will want to bring every influential team member together in a team meeting or collaborative session to make changes to the plan with the goal of accelerating the business and using everyone's skills as they should be used.

[ ] Step 138 -   Schedule a time now to either go over the business plan with your new hire or have a team meeting for everyone to evaluate the business plan together.

Having everyone involved in this process will allow them to "own" the plan. If they own the plan or a part thereof, they are going to be eager to meet the goal or goals you've set.

Team Agreements

Team agreements are incredibly important, but they can be as simple as an email that outlines job requirements, payment, term of employment (if any), and start date. The more detailed the agreement is, the better.

You may be thinking "I don't want to make things really strict because then we'll have a bad working relationship" or "won't that limit their creativity?" Both of these are common myths. A detailed agreement is meant to get all the expectations of both parties in writing and clearly laid out. This is beneficial for both sides because it prevents a bad working relationship. The clear expectations alleviate the stress and friction that results when expectations go unmet.

Legal Tip: Agreements can be written in plain English.

The idea of an agreement such as this is to put down everything the team has talked about and make it so each member can act knowing exactly what will happen in each case. This is important to prevent two types of conversations.

The first conversation you're avoiding is the one that starts with the question of whether or not the person is able to do what he wants to do. If he or she is unable to do what they wanted, this creates strain. The other type of conversation is the one where you have to punish or he asks for forgiveness. This also creates strain. If there are clear expectations, these conversations never come up, or at least come up much less.

The other myth that agreements limit creativity is groundless. The only creativity that should be limited in this agreement, which does not have to be, is the ability to do anything to and with the company.

Your agreement will likely put limits on whether or not this team member can bind the company to certain types of agreements. You can limit or leave open this limitation as much as you'd like. If a certain area of creativity is important, it can be put in the agreement that your team member has free reign to do anything he wants in that particular area. You certainly wouldn't want your team member having free reign to set his salary or equity, but maybe he could have some authority to change how his department is managed as long as certain goals are still maintained. It's up to you, as long as your agreement doesn't violate public policy.

Legal Tip: The agreements that micromanage another team member lead to strained relationships. Clear expectations are different from strict micromanagement.

A detailed agreement can be renegotiated. If the members find that an agreement does not address certain aspects that you're looking to address or it puts too many limits on a certain area, you can always renegotiate. You're the owners and can do whatever you'd like as long as you still maintain that authority in the company. Since you also maintain the right to fire a person, absent giving that right away, you can offer a lower salary to employees in exchange for keeping their job. This isn't the best for building a trusting relationship, but it's how the system works. Changes in equity, however, aren't as free form. Once a person has equity, it cannot be taken away unless that was outlined in the original equity agreement.

Legal Tip: Lowering a person's salary may sometimes result in certain unemployment insurance issues, so be careful with that strategy.

[ ] Step 139 -   Write down any company-wide structural changes that will take place with your new team member.

[ ] Step 140 -   For any changes that do not affect your governing document, member's rights, management, or anything to do with ownership, write down the changes in a Company Policies document.

[ ] Step 141 -   If your company is an LLC, make a draft
Operating Agreement that reflects the changes listed in the
earlier step about structural changes.

[ ] Step 142 -   If your company is a Corporation, make a
draft Bylaws that reflects the changes listed in the step
about structural changes.

Equity Agreements

If you've given your team member equity in exchange for her
service, you will need an equity agreement. Once again, these can
be as simple as an email; however, these agreements are slightly
more complex due to potential securities issues, tax issues, and
investor issues that may come up if you do them wrong.

---

*Tip: If you have a simple exchange of work for equity
arrangement, you may be able to get away with a simple
one-page agreement without the attorney.*

Several organization and clinics will have sample equity
agreements you can use if you feel comfortable using these. This is
one area I'd recommend having a lawyer explain them to you
because of the vast tax, securities, and state law consequences
involved.

If you're able to, find a time when a lawyer is explaining equity
agreements to an audience at some sort of teaching event or seminar.
Even if you don't write them yourself, this is a good idea because
you'll want to understand what these mean and what to look out for
in these agreements.

After learning about these equity agreements, if you feel
comfortable with the sample agreement you got from an
organization, you should go ahead and use that one. Be very wary
of agreements you've found online. Just because it worked for
someone does not mean it will work for you. Additionally, different
states have different laws and this can really cause catastrophic

problems for you down the road. Some of the problems that may occur: (1) tax bills you didn't see coming that you owe personally, (2) investigation by the Securities and Exchange Commission, (3) accidentally giving more equity to your partner than you thought, (4) suddenly getting more or different partners than you bargained for, (5) loss of control of your company, and many other problems.

Tip: We've seen more issues with borrowing another person's equity agreement than those who write their own.

These are complicated agreements and shouldn't be done without regard to the potential consequences. This isn't to say you cannot do them yourself if they're simpler arrangements, but the amount of time you should spend researching them in addition to the potential risk of doing them wrong is a high cost that may justify the hiring of an attorney to do them for you. Fortunately, once you have one agreement, you should be able to use the same agreement for the rest of your equity offers, assuming your attorney set them up in that manner, and the offers are relatively the same.

Expectations in Writing

The main reason you want an equity or team agreement in writing is so your expectations are clearly laid out. It is a waste of time to have to revisit a person's role each and every time something comes up. This micromanaging is not an effective use of your time. Any time you're spending explaining expectations is time you are not using to build the company.

Even if you verbally explained all the expectations in the first meeting, six months down the road, the memory will have warped in your mind, as well as the mind of your team member. Therefore, your expectations may not be lined up anymore, which is why putting them in writing is always best.

Expectations should include percentage, scope of work, and any deadlines or other measurements. If you think back to our SMART goals section, this is a good application for some of those.

| [ ] Step 143 - Write down any requirements you will need in your equity agreements.

| [ ] Step 144 - If you're drafting the equity agreement yourself, write that now.

Note: We're having you draft an equity agreement before discussing all the provisions so you cover the basics well.

Vesting

One of the first features you'll likely want to consider in an equity agreement is the possibility of vesting. This simply means that the percent of equity you've given your partner will not become fully effective until after a certain date. This is most common when a partner is contributing something over time, like labor. Because not all of her contribution is made up front, she should not be entitled to full rights up front. Vesting is a protection for current partners who have already contributed something of value to the company. Cash contributions are typically not subject to vesting unless the cash investment is made over time.

Review of Work Completed

Some owners like to put in a requirement that the work be reviewed and accepted before giving any sort of equity to the partner. You can do this, and it switches the legal burden off of you, but is one of those subjective areas that can lead to conflict. It is better to find someone you can trust.

Buyout Clause

A buyout clause is something you may be interested in including, but if done in a one-sided fashion, you're likely going to scare away good talent. A buyout clause is a provision that you include to give the original or majority owner the right to buy back the equity in the company. This could be at a set price, after a valuation, some multiple of cash flow, or upon some event or deadline. As long as they're not seemingly fraudulent, these are typically enforceable, but keep in mind that including this clause may also have tax consequences.

Author's Note: We rarely include these in our documents because they scare away talented entrepreneurs who otherwise would join the team.

Loss of Control

Anytime you give up equity, you give up some control. Even "non-controlling" shares have some level of control over what happens to their shares and the company as a whole. Fortunately, you do have the ability to create this distinction between controlling and non-controlling shares in both a corporation and an LLC.

Tip: Talk to an attorney or CPA before having multiple share types if you want to be taxed as an S Corp. There are limitations that may prevent you from doing so.

If you gave everyone the same level of control that you have, you'd have to involve each member in important decisions like appointment of management or issuance of employee stock options. This includes silent investors, employees, and lower-ranked partners. This would create a level of bureaucracy that you would likely not want to deal with.

Some partners will only work for controlling shares and therefore you would have to give up some major portions of control of your company. Others will take non-controlling shares, but instead will put limitations on how you run the company. Professional investors are notorious for putting strings on how you run the company and they do so in their equity agreements.

In any equity agreement, they'll require you to do things that protect their interest. You have to give up the ability to freely control your company. The good news is that most professional investors who put strings on the management of the company put restrictions that ultimately help the company. They may make it harder to run the company in your way, but the company itself will likely do better.

IPO Considerations

If your ultimate goal could involve an initial public offering (IPO), you would want to keep that in mind when drafting the equity agreements. You will need several additions, including limitations on the ability to sell right after an IPO, included in your agreements to protect your company from investigations by the SEC and devaluation or artificial inflation of the cost of your stock.

An IPO is when a private company becomes publicly available for trading on a stock market like the NYSE or NASDAQ. It is a very complicated process, but for the right companies, it can be incredibly lucrative.

Transferability

You will want to put limits on the transferability of your equity from your partner to other people or companies. The reason for this mostly revolves around your desire to not work with strangers. Presumably, you did a lot of work ensuring that your team member is someone you can work with in a good relationship. Having a random person in your company would make all of that for naught.

Another reason you want to restrict transfers because certain ownership interests are not allowed to be freely transferable without being registered with the SEC. Any free transfer in violation of this could result in fines and investigations.

Furthermore, some entities have restrictions on ownership of the company. If you have one of these entities and you suddenly exceed the number or have the wrong type of owners, you would be forced into a restructuring of the company and could face unfavorable tax or legal consequences.

You cannot fully restrict transfer of ownership interest, but you can include things like a right of first refusal in certain areas. Be careful if you choose to do this yourself. This restriction on transfer can also be included in your company's operating agreement, if your company is an LLC. In corporations, you would include this in the equity agreements.

Your Partner's Spouse

The problem with not having restrictions on transfers is the whole "partner's spouse" dilemma. The classic example of what happens if you don't have clear transfer restrictions is the possibility of you ending up working with your partner's spouse (or ex-spouse) when your partner dies, gets divorced, or otherwise leaves the ownership to his spouse.

It isn't always the spouse, either. You may see friends, family, or creditors that you've never met or heard of suddenly becoming owners just like you.

In death, your partner will leave all his assets to whomever he lists in his will or according to the intestacy laws of his state. This is typically going to start with spouse and children, but can branch out into charities, grandchildren, cousins, friends, caretakers, and organizations. This could wind up being a big group of people owning your company, and furthermore, some entities have a limit on how many owners they can have as well as what types of entities are allowed to own that company. You may be forced into restructuring simply because your partner dies and you didn't have an enforceable buy back clause in place.

If your partner gets a divorce, all of his assets are subject to the divorce estate. This means his spouse may be able to take his ownership of the company. Sometimes, this may include only half of his ownership in the company, so you may find yourself acting as a marriage counselor instead of doing your job. Nobody wants this.

What can you do if your partner leaves and doesn't continue to work for or with the company? The default rule is nothing. She's already earned her percentage of the company and therefore can do whatever she likes. If you establish ongoing requirements, you would be able to set up a system that allows buy back if the other person is inactive or not doing her job.

Keep in mind that each limitation or requirement devalues the equity you are giving and may lessen how much your partner will want to take the offer and work with you.

Something Agreeable

You can add all the legal and favorable terms you'd like, but the important thing to remember is that this is a relationship. You're working with another person, and you're going to need to craft something that is agreeable to both parties. You don't want one side to be offended or walk away when you present the offer, so it has to be reasonable enough that she will accept or take the opportunity to negotiate the deal.

Incentives Instead of Punishments

Some companies like to provide incentives for meeting certain deadlines instead of punishments for missing them. This is a stronger way of doing things. It changes the psychology of the arrangement. The number they see will be the number without the incentives which motivates them less, but they will see bonuses which we interpret differently than salaries. A lot of people like working for bonuses instead of a straight salary because it has the "prize value" associated with it. People would much rather pay the same amount to win a $5 stuffed bear at a fair than they would like to buy a $20 stuffed bear in the store, even though they spent $20 getting the $5 bear. Why? Because of the prize value. It's worth more because you earned it.

The person under the deadline will also be under less stress to meet the deadlines which allows them to work with a clearer head. As long as they aren't a natural procrastinator, this will allow them to work more efficiently and finish earlier.

Different methods work for different people. There's no reason you can't create some hybrid approach, but you should be conscious of the effects you're trying to have and the effects you are actually having through your approach.

Strangely enough, we've also discovered that most people assume they'll obtain virtually every incentive bonus. This keeps the contract value high to them, but makes them disappointed when the bonus is missed. Like other areas of contracts, be careful. You want to set up a system where they're set up to succeed, not fail. You also want to ensure that you're transparent about the relationship. Anything hidden is a source of conflict.

[ ] Step 145 -   If you're having an attorney draft your equity agreements, have the attorney draft that agreement now. If you wrote this agreement yourself, go back and make changes based on what you now know.

Communication

No matter what, you have to make sure you communicate. Communication can be done in person, over email, on the phone or any other way in which you both can get your ideas out of your head and to the other person. Some people still utilize postal mail more than any other medium, and this is perfectly fine as long as both parties agree to it.

Communication is the most important part of any relationship. There's no other way to maintain a relationship other than through communication in some form because a relationship is merely the communication between two people.

Scheduled Meetings

You should have regularly scheduled meetings, either in person or over the phone, where you can check up on progress, learn of any concerns or problems, and hear the positives of the relationship.

It's also important to use part of this time to be social, building up trust in each other. People inherently like to like other people. As we continue to engage with others, we tend to gravitate toward liking them. This isn't always true, but it's a fairly good guideline. If you've vetted the person properly, this will almost always be true in your team member's case because you share values and trust.

You may be tempted to brush off these regular meetings, but they're some of the more important meetings you have. They're the primary way to ensure you always have a good working relationship with your team and that things are going well. If a team member is working on something project-based, this also provides a reminder to work on it more or seek help when needed.

Companies are pass-through entities when it comes to excitement and emotions. For example, if you are disinterested during these meetings, your team member will also become disinterested in the project they are working on, as well as the company as a whole. If you're excited during these meetings, you'll pass on your energy to your team member and they will be excited as well. It's your job, as the owner, to provide guidance on what emotion to feel, and it will trickle down into every aspect of the company.

[ ] Step 146 -   Determine when your scheduled team meetings will be and schedule the first few months.

Memos

"The difference between science and screwing around is documentation." – Adam Savage, Mythbusters

Very few people love memos, but they're important. Memos provide a standardized way to communicate companywide that is easy to scan and easy to quickly access information. They provide the history of the company and projects, which are vital for institutional memory.

A memo does not have to be fancy. All it needs is a From, To, Date, and Reason (RE) header followed by the message. Each memo ends with a call to action and the signature.

The message itself starts with a sentence describing why the memo is being written. That sentence is followed by a summary of the findings and then a longer description of the findings. Typically, you're only going to need to read the intro, the summary of the findings and the call to action because these are the most important parts; that is the reason memos are so useful.

[ ] Step 147 -   Create the standardized memo template for your company to use.

Fortunately for you, emails look exactly like a memo. The important thing is remembering to format the content like memo. Imagine cycling through three thousand emails from the one person trying to find your answer from six months ago. If you had the summaries as you should, the first sentence would be all you need to know to figure out if this is the right email. In emails, it's also important to change the subject line. Even when you reply, make sure the subject line is appropriate to the message.

Memos exist to save you and the managers work. Memos may be a little more work for the lower level employees, but when you save time, your company saves time. Furthermore, the memo format takes seconds to make. Once you get used to them, they're second nature.

Project Management Software

Keeping track of your projects should not be done in your mind. You need systems in place to record and assess how things are going. Project management software is incredibly useful as far as keeping things organized and having one depository for all of the information. You will want to use the one that meets the requirements for your project.

Different industries have more customized software specific to industry needs, so it is important to do some research and test the best options. There are also a wide variety of prices for the software out there, so that's another consideration you should have prior to picking which one works for you.

[ ] Step 148 -   Research and select the project management tool you want to use.

Write Everything Down

Write absolutely everything down. Companies are only as strong as their records. The goal is to ensure that if anything happens to you, your company would be able to keep running.

The purpose of writing things down is so you have consistency. When you first start the company, you do everything. If you write everything down, you will already have the training manual for your first hire because your first hire is going to take away some of the responsibility that you carried. This keeps happening as you hire more people. The consistent records make for minimal training time and more consistency. Your customers and employees will love the consistency and your company will become a more efficient machine.

People assume death is the only way that they could leave the company, but that's rarely the thing that stops you from running your company. You may suffer a serious injury, want to retire, have to move for a different career, and more. In these cases, your company should be able to keep moving along either paying you dividends or having been sold. As you've created value in this company, you should get value out of it when you leave.

[ ] Step 149 -   Document any decisions you've made in this process regarding organization-wide policies or software.

CHAPTER 15 - EMPLOYEES

Legal Requirements to Having Employees

If your company wants employees, you're going to have to ensure that you follow a strict set of rules. For most new companies, it's far more advisable to hire independent contractors or avoid hiring employees for as long as possible. It isn't a headache once everything is in place, but noncompliance with the rules can result in large fines and penalties through the Department of Labor and IRS.

It may be a good idea to bring in a human resources expert or employment lawyer early on to ensure that compliance is met. The fines and penalties are far more costly than this expert and they help you spot things you never expected. If you're a DIY-er, you can try to do the research yourself, as there are plenty of guides provided by the Department of Labor and IRS to help.

Payroll compliance issues are among the most common problems a business owners faces. For that reason, you should be very careful or seek the help of others to remain compliant.

Employee Versus Independent Contractor

The first important consideration is whether your hire is an employee or an independent contractor. The IRS looks to three factors when determining if a worker is an employee or an independent contractor. The factors are behavioral, financial, and type of relationship. None of these factors are clearly black and white; rather, they fit on a sliding scale.

Behavioral. Does the company control or have the right to control what the worker does and how the worker does his or her job? Put simply, how much guidance is there on how the job gets done? The less creativity and control over how the job gets done (not what job gets done), the less likely he is an independent contractor.

Here are some things in the behavioral aspect that you can do to make it more likely that your hire is an independent contractor:

- Provide guidelines on outcome, not how to get there. (i.e. don't give step by step processes on how to do the job, but rather the desired outcome of the job).
- Don't provide instructions on what equipment to use unless it makes a difference in the outcome.
- Don't provide instructions on who to hire.
- Don't provide instructions on where to purchase supplies/services.
- Don't provide training. Training implies an employee relationship and an ongoing one.

Financial. Are the business aspects of the worker's job controlled by the payer? This factor is a numbers game, but without any fixed amounts to make the determination. The IRS will look to whether, because of financial contributions and control, the hire appears to be an employee or an independent contractor. There are several very noticeable differences between employee-employer relationships versus that of an independent contractor. For example, a photographer who is an employee will use the camera supplied by the company rather than use his or her own. Likewise, independent contractors are not reimbursed for numerous expenses, unlike an employee who might have had to pay out-of-pocket.

Some things to look at in this factor:

- Significant investment: if the tools provided are owned by the hire, they're more likely an independent contractor.
- Unreimbursed expenses: employees are more likely to be reimbursed.
- Opportunity for profit or loss: instead of a fixed hourly wage, if there's an opportunity to make more or make less because of financial decisions, the worker is more likely an independent contractor. An employee will never face the opportunity to make a loss.

- Services available to the market: Employees can be restricted from working in the general market, but independent contractors must be allowed to advertise, maintain a visible business location and take on other clients.
- Method of payment: Guaranteed payment over salary or hourly wage makes a case for employee, but flat fee per job is more likely an independent contractor.

Type of Relationship. Are there written contracts or employee type benefits? Will the relationship continue, and is the work performed a key aspect of the business? This is another loose test for the IRS. There is no set criteria that will upset an employee or independent contractor relationship. The IRS will look to the contract, the nature of the business relationship, and subjective features that cannot be measured in the other two factors.

It's important to know that what the contract says to this extent has **no** bearing on the IRS's determination. If the contract says the hire is an independent contractor, yet fits into the definition of an employee, the IRS will determine that hire is an employee and will treat him or her as such for tax purposes.

Some key things to look at under this factor:

- Employee benefits are only for employees. You cannot offer insurance, pension plans, paid vacation, sick days, etc. to an independent contractor. It's just not possible so any inclusion of these things in an agreement makes the person an employee, if they're validly included.
- Permanency of the Relationship. If you hire a worker expecting an indefinite relationship rather than a per-job relationship, you're looking at an employee. To better position yourself to hire an independent contractor, make clear in the contract and in the relationship that his is a hire specifically for one job. You can always renegotiate another contract for the next job.
- Services provided as key activities of the business. In a grocery store context, since making sales is a key activity of the business, it is more likely that a cashier is an employee than an independent contractor. This piece of the determination is not very weighted because of the nature of

business now. It is actually quite common for bartenders at bars, doctors at hospitals, lawyers in law firms, and other people who are the key component of a business to be independent contractors. The core functions of your business can be separated and contracted out, but it must be done properly.

For additional reading on the IRS determination, see the IRS's website: https://www.irs.gov/Businesses/Small-Businesses-&-Self-Employed/Independent-Contractor-Self-Employed-or-Employee

---

Additionally, each state's Department of Labor and the Federal Department of Labor has their own guidelines as well. Just because your hire is classified as an independent contractor for IRS purposes does not mean that she is an independent contractor under your state law. Employees have different requirements in the Department of Labor; therefore, you must be careful to ensure you know exactly where your hire lies. If you have any doubt, you should seek the help of a reputable employment lawyer, human resources expert, or ask for a determination from the IRS or DOL.

The United States Supreme Court has held the following factors to be significant, but not exclusive:

1. The extent to which the services rendered are an integral part of the principal's business;
2. The permanency of the relationship;
3. The amount of the alleged contractor's investment in facilities and equipment;
4. The nature and degree of control by the principal;
5. The alleged contractor's opportunities for profit and loss;
6. The amount of initiative, judgment, or foresight in open market competition with others required for the success of the claimed independent contract; and
7. The degree of independent business organization and operation.

Remember, failure to classify properly through the IRS could result in penalties and back FICA taxes and payment of back withholdings. Failure to classify properly through the Department of Labor can result in many penalties, fines and back wages to the employee. The IRS is looking out for the IRS, but the Department of Labor is there to protect the employees.

> [ ] Step 150 -   Make the determination for any employees or independent contractors to ensure they're properly classified. If you cannot make the determination yourself, seek the guidance of a professional.

Unemployment Insurance

Any employer with employees is required to pay the unemployment insurance tax. Unemployment Insurance protects employees who have lost their jobs at no fault of their own. Employers pay the federal and state level tax on the first $7,000 of earnings that each employee makes. That money is saved in trust until it is needed for when that employer has unemployment issues.

> [ ] Step 151 -   If you have employees, set up your unemployment insurance account with your state.

Workers' Compensation

The Workers' Compensation Act requires that any employer who employs employees provide workers' compensation coverage. Any sole proprietor or partner of a business whose employees are eligible for benefits may also be covered as an employee, but is not included in the number that are counted for required coverage. The number of employees may vary, but in North Carolina, if you have 3 or more employees, or are in certain industries, you're required to carry workers' compensation insurance. No matter what, it is a good idea to carry when you have employees.

> [ ] Step 152 -   If you have employees, obtain workers' compensation insurance for them.

Withholdings

When you hire employees, you're required to withhold federal and state taxes. This includes state income taxes, federal income taxes, and the Federal Social Security and Medicare taxes.

The incomes taxes are withheld directly from the employee's paycheck each pay period, or from self-employed person's pay on a monthly or quarterly basis.

The Social Security and Medicare taxes, or FICA tax, is the Federal Insurance Contributions Act tax. This amount is paid half by the employer and half by the employee. In the case of a self-employed individual, you will pay both halves, with one half being deductible from your personal taxes.

The standard rate for FICA is 6.2% to Social Security and 1.45% to Medicare for each half of the tax. The Social Security portion has a cap on how much of a person's income is taxed whereas the Medicare tax has no upper limit.

Employers can set up an online account with the Electronic Federal Tax Payment System to make it easier to make the online payments for each employee and for themselves.

Additionally, payroll companies will do this entire process for you. Because of the complexities of withholdings and the large penalties if you do it wrong, it is advisable to have a payroll system set up with your bank or a separate payroll company. This not only helps ensure you do it right, but also saves you time that you should be spending on your company instead. What would take you hours each week takes your payroll company only a few minutes to do.

Tip: Payroll companies range from $30 to hundreds. Shopping around could save you a significant amount of money. Banks rarely provide the cheapest solution.

To determine how much money to withhold, your employee must complete form W-4 (and state equivalent), and you must keep this on file and provide to your payroll company, if you have one.

[ ] Step 153 -   Start an employment folder in your computer file system. Put the W-4, state equivalent, and any other employment documents you've made in there.

Tip: In NC, the state equivalent to the W-4 is the <u>NC-4</u>.

[ ] Step 154 -   Complete your own W-4 and state equivalent withholdings worksheet.

Tip: The W-4 can be found on the IRS website by searching for W-4.

<u>https://www.irs.gov/uac/About-Form-W4</u>

Garnishment

Sometimes, employers are required to garnish their employees' wages for things like alimony, child support and judicial orders. When you get these orders, you must comply as long as they come from the government; otherwise, you may be held liable for the full amount of the garnishment. These orders are no joke, and shouldn't be taken as a joke. Failure to comply with the juridical orders can result in fines, penalties, sanctions, and a plethora of other punishments.

Human Resources Requirements

There are a large number of requirements that you must follow in order to prevent employee issues, harassment complaints, department of labor violations, and lackluster record keeping. Sba.gov contains a lot of great articles on how to ensure that your company complies with all of the human resources requirements out there, but to be safe, it may be best to hire someone to handle this aspect of your company as well.

Fair Hiring Methodologies

When hiring your employees, you must ensure to maintain the fairest methods for choosing who to hire. Obviously, you cannot turn someone away because of their gender, race, skin color, national origin, age, sex, pregnancy, citizenship, religion, veteran status or genetic information. Any other immutable traits should also be avoided when doing your hiring.

Some people make hiring decisions based on weight and attractiveness. These should be avoided, not because of legal requirements (yet), but because any level of discrimination based on immutable traits creates waste in the marketplace. Any inefficiency will hurt your company and should be avoided.

There are some exceptions to these rules. For example, casting for a particular role in a movie may require specific characteristics, but even then, think about whether it matters. In the 2014 movie "Annie," the producers took an historically white role and cast an African American child instead. Ultimately, the race of the child did not matter to make the story work.

You should take great care to ensure to hire the best person for the job, and not base your decision on any other characteristic or factor. Remember earlier when we discussed the four questions when hiring? If they meet the criteria, they are a good candidate.

Occupational Safety and Health Act

We've all heard of OSHA, but do we know what the requirements are? There are a significant number of very specific requirements that must be followed. Many of these requirements are industry specific or situational. Fortunately for you, OSHA provides a ton of resources as well as on site consultations by OSHA consultants.

The OSHA consultants are completely separate from the compliance department. They're around to help ensure you have the tools and knowledge necessary to create a safe working environment. Be sure to take advantage of this resource. In North Carolina, you call 1-800-NC-LABOR for more information.

Other resources can be found on osha.gov.

[ ] Step 155 -   If you have any sort of heavy machinery, chemicals, or other things that could kill an employee or customer, call your OSHA Department and find out what your requirements are.

Employment Eligibility Verification

Every employee that you hire needs to have a Form I-9. This form is used to verify the identity and employment authorization. This includes both citizens and noncitizens. This is the form that includes proof of identity and employment authorization. You will then be responsible for keeping this form on file for a designated period of time in case it needs to be inspected.

[ ] Step 156 -   Add the I-9 to your employment folder on your computer.

Tip: The I-9 can be found on the US Citizenship and Immigration Services website:

https://www.uscis.gov/i-9

CHAPTER 16 - EMPLOYEE HANDBOOK

If you have employees or are planning on having employees anytime soon, the next document you're going to need to compile is the employee handbook. You should have this before you have employees, not after. As soon as you're thinking about getting employees, create this. For most entrepreneurs, you're already thinking of getting employees before you start your business. It's best to have something minimal on hand, just in case.

It's common that by the time you want an employee, you're too swamped to properly interview the person, much less draft up an employee handbook.

Employee handbooks contain all the information your employee needs to know about working in the company, but nothing about the production the company does. (That's in the standard operating procedure.) So, every employee should be quite familiar with both the employee handbook (guide to being an employee) and the standard operating procedure (guide to getting things done).

Each employee handbook contains a lot of the same information, like nondiscrimination policies, dispute resolution, timesheets, etc., but your employee handbook is also a great opportunity to reflect on company values and build a corporate culture.

Free From The Society of Human Resource Management on www.shrm.org

We're not big fans on reinventing the wheel, and although the handbook terms Law Plus Plus use are much different from the Society for Human Resource Management's employee handbook, theirs is simpler for DIY customization, especially in multiple states.

You can pay a lot for a custom built employee handbook, and they're worth the price when you can afford it, but if you're short on cash or just want the basics, check out www.shrm.gov. On that site, there are a lot of great resources, including an employee handbook, with some state-specific information.

> [ ] Step 157 -   Download SHRM's employee handbook to your employment folder on your computer at https://www.shrm.org/templatestools/samples/pages/emplo yeehandbook.aspx or hire someone to make a handbook for you. If you hired someone to make the handbook for you, skip all the remaining steps in this chapter.

> [ ] Step 158 -   Fill in your company name wherever it is necessary in the handbook you just downloaded.

Even if you hired someone to write the handbook for you, you should understand its content.

"At Will" Versus "For Term"

By default, in most states, employees are at-will employees, meaning that they can be fired at any time for any nondiscriminatory reason. If you think you might be violating an anti-discriminatory law, you should check with your attorney.

> [ ] Step 159 -   Write down every type of position (manager, sales, etc.) and whether those positions are for term or at-will, as well as what requirements they have. You should already have most of this information from the "Building the Team" section.

Dispute Procedure

Your employee handbook should have dispute procedures in case of harassment, mismanagement, or any other dispute that may arise. If you have a human resources director, that person should be in charge of handling these disputes, unless, of course, that person is the focus of the dispute.

As courts have an appeal process, so should your complaint procedure. If the employee gets a bad decision from the human resources director, or whoever else she reports to, she should have a second level to appeal that decision. This appeal should be very similar to how appellate courts work in the United States, only reviewing the whole case if the employee can prove there was a mistake made in the first case, not just disappointment with the decision.

Keep in mind that your employee can still always quit or take your company to court regardless of the outcome. You can include in the handbook that she may only file suit against your company after exhausting the internal complaint, and that might protect you to a limited degree. Employees never waive their right to sue for harassment, discrimination, or a hostile work environment, no matter what you've put in the handbook.

When dealing with a complaint or any sort of dispute, you need to record all of the facts and get a signed statement from the employee. These records are vital to protecting yourself. In a court, if you can demonstrate a fair attempt at resolving the issue, your company will be far less likely to suffer harm. If, however, you cannot prove anything, the Department of Labor and courts frequently side with the employee.

You should also record any decision and why the decision was made. Any records made for these disputes should be kept on hand for at least ten years if not indefinitely. You want to make sure that the statute of limitations has completely run before destroying any records of employee disputes or complaints.

[ ] Step 160 -   Check the complaint procedure in the sample handbook and make any changes you see fit.

How to Treat Customers/Clients

If your employees interact with customers, you'll want a detailed section on expectations when working with the customers or clients. This section should reflect the values and the brand of the company.

No matter what, there should be a statement to the effect that the customers are the reason for the business and they should be treated with respect, that customers should not be harassed, and any complaints against the employee for harassment or mistreatment would be taken very seriously. Such complaints, if proven to be true, may be grounds for termination or suspension without pay.

Vendor Relationships

Many people get the misconception that because you're paying someone or doing a favor for them, you do not need to treat that person with respect. It is, however, important to keep good relationships with everyone you work with. This includes vendors or service providers. Any tension in your company creates friction and therefore, creates waste.

> [ ] Step 161 -   Add a policy in the Expectations section for how to treat customers and vendors.

Dress Code

"Dress for the job you want" is a great principle for the employee level. For the employer, you should set your policy in a way that reflects your company culture. If you run a laid back company, set the dress code as laid back. If you're formal and your customers expect formal, set your dress code as formal. No matter what, however, you should have some level of dress code.

> [ ] Step 162 -   Read the dress code in the sample handbook and make any changes you want.

Anti-Discrimination Policy

If you maintain an anti-discrimination policy, it is very important to include it in your employee handbook. Most companies are required to maintain this policy to some degree, but even exempt companies may want to as a part of the company.

Upon the principle that immutable characteristics do not impact a person's ability to do quality work in any given field, discrimination lowers your chances of getting the most qualified applicant for the position you're trying to fulfill because it narrows your search field.

Look at this simple scenario:

You're hiring for a retail clerk and you have 120 applicants. If you hire from this full pool of applicants, you have a 120/120 or 100% chance of interviewing the best applicant. Let's change the scenario and say that 65 of the applicants are women and you decide you do not want a woman for this role. In that case, you have a 55/120 or 46% chance of interviewing the best applicant.

This works for any immutable characteristic. Though the numbers vary, eliminating any classification of people from your pool will lower your chances of finding the best applicant. Even if the pool of applicants was the size of the entire world population or as small as an inter-departmental hiring, the concept remains the same.

Furthermore, any loss of chance to get the best applicant, if extrapolated to a company as a whole throughout its lifespan, will create massive inefficiencies. In our free-market economy, we know that inefficiencies destroy companies, and discrimination is no different. Companies that maintain discriminatory policies slowly die.

Sometimes, companies that maintain discriminatory policies quickly die when they are sued for discriminatory firing or for maintaining a hostile workplace. This is just one of many reasons to not discriminate, and therefore, the policy should be written down, taken to heart, and constantly reinforced to all employees, especially any employees that make personnel decisions.

[ ] Step 163 -   Read through the sample anti-discrimination policy and make any changes you see fit. It is best not to remove any portions, but you can add more and make the protections stronger.

Benefits

If your company offers benefits like health insurance, life insurance, 401k, etc., you will want to list them in the employee handbook. This serves as a guide for your employees on how to take advantage of these benefits, or if any of the benefits are automatic.

Your list of benefits may be extensive and you may want to refer the employee to another location to get all of the information. That is fine to do, but you should at least reference the broad areas of benefits you offer because this is part of the agreement you have with your employee and it will be more enticing for them to join your company seeing all of these available. It also counterbalances the handbook from being completely one-sided. Having only rules and regulations within the handbook will encourage your employees to glaze over it instead of fully reading its content.

If any of the benefits require withholdings from an employee's paycheck, these are absolutely required by law to be listed with how much the withholding will be.

[ ] Step 164 - List any benefits your company offers in the handbook, how to enroll in them, and the costs associated with the benefits. If you cannot list a specific cost, list how the cost is determined.

Compensation

Employees love to know what they get paid, and although the handbook will be standardized, you want to put as much detail about compensation in it as possible. You obviously won't list their exact salary; however, you can list generalities about their compensation.

[ ] Step 165 - In the handbook, read through the compensation section, filling in any blanks, and making any changes you see fit.

Getting Paid

What employees typically care about most is how they're going to get paid. If you pay your employees, you should include how they get paid. Be sure to include how often and what method. If you have electronic deposits, let them know how to sign up. If you have paper checks, let them know where to pick them up or how they'll receive them.

You also want to include any information about deductions and withholdings for state, local and federal taxes as well as any special deductions you might have. If you don't get them to agree to specific deductions from their paycheck, yet make the deductions anyway, you could face penalties from the Department of Labor. Even if you think the employee stole money from a cash register, you can't withhold it from the paycheck without their prior agreement. (In this case, call the police.)

Include Taxes

You should also include which taxes your employee will be responsible for. For income taxes, you'll be required to withhold the taxes from your employees' paychecks. You should include how this is calculated, where the money goes and how to change the information for tax purposes in case anything changes.

FICA

FICA tax is something commonly misunderstood by employees. It includes social security tax and Medicare, but the employee is only responsible for paying one half out of his or her paycheck. The other half is paid by the employer. You should include how and why your employee's half is deducted from his paycheck. This explanation will help eliminate confusion should there be an issue later on down the road. You should also include how the other half is paid by the company, alluding to your employee that you're both in this tax together.

Withholdings for Garnishment

Many states allow the garnishment of wages for court judgments. Even if your state doesn't allow it, you should put in something regarding the fact that if a court demands that you garnish wages, you will be complying. Put this in just in case the law changes and your state later allows it. You want to be proactive with your employee handbook.

Certain things, such as back alimony and child support, are almost always allowed to be taken as a garnishment of wages. Having a blanket statement allowing you to garnish wages by order of any court would cover you more than trying to separate out every circumstance that may come up.

Furthermore, the IRS and the State's Department of Revenue will be allowed to garnish wages for unpaid taxes and penalties. Be sure to include something to the extent that allows you to garnish for these government agencies.

What happens if you do not garnish? Whatever you do, make sure you comply with the IRS, State Department of Revenue and the

Courts. If you don't, there are many provisions that may result in your company becoming solely responsible for the garnishment amount along with potential fines and penalties.

So, what happens if you don't let your employee know, yet you still withhold? If you do this, you may actually be subject to fines from the Department of Labor for failure to get permission and failure to notify your employee of a deduction from his paycheck.

The moral of the story is that you must include that you're allowed to make deductions from your employee's paycheck for garnishments from the Courts, IRS and Department of Revenue, or you may be subject to fines or even the whole cost of the debt to be garnished.

Withholdings for Retirement

Many companies like to help employees save for retirement with 401ks, IRAs, Pensions and more. If your company offers retirement plans, you must either include these policies in the handbook or in a separate agreement to withhold the wages to fund the retirement. Once again, you're withholding payments so, as a business owner, you don't want to risk a Department of Labor investigation. Department of Labor fines can be very costly, and the investigation can be time-consuming. You would save yourself a lot of risk by including this in your handbook from the start and avoiding the possibility before it comes up.

Withholdings for Benefits

If you offer benefits for your employees that they have to pay a portion of, you need to make that clear in the employee handbook. It's the same thing as any other withholding: it must be done in writing before the deduction is taken out. If the employee clearly understands the deduction, then that will protect you from her filing a complaint with the department of labor. Even if she does file a complaint, having the withholding in writing before the withholding is taken out will protect you in that case, as that is the proper procedure.

[ ] Step 166 -   Go through the Compensation section knowing what you know now and add any provisions regarding withholdings, taxes, or other compensation matters you want to include.

Tip: Department of Labor investigations are costly and time-consuming. Avoiding them through good relations with your employees is by far the best strategy. Be proactive because any scent of wrongdoing on your part and the Department of Labor investigator will have the authority to expand the investigation to other employees and your company as a whole.

Workers' Compensation Laws

You should include in the handbook the workers' compensation laws, and you should ensure you understand what these mean for your company.

If a worker is injured on the job through the negligence of the employer, she can recover medical costs as well as the replacement of wages during the time she was unable to work.

In the handbook, you'll want to provide the procedure for making a claim as well as explaining that a successful claim relinquishes the employee's right to sue the employer. Not having workers' compensation insurance can subject the company to fines and penalties if that company has employees.

Work Schedules

Determining when an employee works is also of great importance to the employee and should be included in the employee handbook. Work schedules provide the outline for when an employee is going to be expected to work, but you can make it flexible enough to allow for changed circumstances.

[ ] Step 167 -   Set up a system for how you determine work schedules, if you have varying schedules.

Standards of Conduct

Set your expectations high and people will be eager to meet them. Some of the more successful companies tell their new hires that they only hire the best and therefore, they expect that they continue to be the best. If you've set up your standards of conduct in such a way that you're suggesting that by operating in this way, they're simply carrying on an already established reputation, your employees will be far more likely to uphold those standards.

Of course, your standards cannot be unreasonable or go against an employee's values. Your hiring process is crucial for ensuring that the employees you hire all share the same values as your company.

[ ] Step 168 -   In your handbook's Expectations section, set any standards for conduct you might have. If the standards already set in the handbook are enough, you can leave them as is.

OSHA Information

The Occupational Safety and Health Administration (OSHA) has many strict rules regarding the workplace and how work is done. A lot of this information is also industry-specific and must be included in the employee handbook. OSHA requires that the employer notify the employees of their rights through posted notices and through notices in the handbook. In order to avoid fines and penalties, you will want to include any pertinent OSHA information in your employee handbook.

Many states, including North Carolina, have free resources that you can use to determine what notices you need in your handbook, on site, and what other requirements you need to fulfill in your industry, location, or size.

Termination Process

The number one reason that employers get sued by their

employees is because something upset the employee. One of the primary reasons employees get upset is because they were terminated in such a way that left them feeling cheated, betrayed or undignified.

If, however, you set up a standard process in your handbook for how terminations will occur and why they occur, your employees will be far less disgruntled when it happens because you followed the procedure and their expectations were met throughout the process. This doesn't mean that they're going to be happy with the outcome, but it will at least leave them with fewer reasons to be upset.

Also, by writing this process down, you will be forced to think about how a poor termination process might come back to hurt the company. Being forced to think about this process will only make it better and eliminate some of the potential liability the company may face.

[ ] Step 169 -   If your employees are not at-will employees, go back and write in their contracts why they may be terminated.

[ ] Step 170 -   For all at-will employees, you should set up a system that outlines how you handle terminations. This is an internal process, not something you put in the handbook.

Tip: Uniformity helps avoid claims of discrimination or wrongful treatment in the termination process.

[ ] Step 171 -   In the compensation section of the handbook, change the annual reviews to something more frequent. The more often, the better for your company's performance and legal safety.

Legal Tip: Regular documented performance reviews with performance plans help in the event you're contesting an

unemployment claim or wrongful termination claim.
Showing that the employee failed to meet a performance
goal set in prior months shows for-cause termination,
unless of course, it was a bad performance goal.

Background Checks

If it makes sense for your company to do background checks, you should include information about how the checks are conducted and when they are conducted in the employee handbook. Put your employees on notice so they'll know what to expect and why they won't get hired if anything problematic shows up.

If your background check includes a credit check, but sure to let your prospective employee know that they have a right to view the contents of the credit report that you've obtained.

These background checks and credit checks can be, and should be, done through a third party because they'll typically cover all of the requirements when it comes to notices and proper procedure.

[ ] Step 172 -   Read through the Background and Reference Checks section of the handbook and make any changes you see fit.

Drug Policy and Testing

If you have a drug policy or require your prospective employees or current employees to submit to drug testing, you will need that in your employee handbook, and it would be even better if you put this in an additional agreement that the employee signs.

Having the drug policy in both places is just added protection for you when and if an employee needs to be fired for failing a drug test. You do not want an employee refuse to get drug tested and then fight a legal battle with you when you fire them for refusing. If it is in both places, your employee will be far less likely to refuse and far less likely to try to fight you if she gets fired.

Furthermore, if you make it absolutely clear this is a condition for employment, you'll be protected if the situation does get in front of a court. This will save you a lot of hassle and money.

[ ] Step 173 -   Go through the drug policy portion of the handbook and make any changes you want to include.

[ ] Step 174 -   Write a separate drug policy that you will have the employee sign. Add this drug policy to the employment folder on your computer.

Unions

In some states, you can require union membership as a condition for employment, but in others you cannot. Be sure to know what your state laws mandate before setting this up.

Furthermore, sometimes unions will negotiate policies for you and your company to follow. If a union you are working with has these additional policies, you'll want to include those in your employee handbook as well.

[ ] Step 175 -   Add whatever union policies you may have.

Safety and Security Procedures

The employee handbook is the best place to include information on what to do in case of fire, natural disaster, terrorism and other safety and security procedures. These safety and security procedures are important to protect your employees and prevent lawsuits for harm caused during a disaster.

If you have multiple buildings or locations, you will have to make your safety and security procedures general or create a different handbook for each location because you will include how to exit the building, if exiting the building is necessary, where to gather, how to conduct headcounts, and enough information to cover as many foreseeable situations that may occur. For example, a manufacturing plant that handles toxic waste will have toxic waste spills included in their handbook; however, a CPA firm will not have to worry about such a disaster.

[ ] Step 176 -   Read through the Safety portion of the handbook and make any necessary changes to reflect your safety procedures.

[ ] Step 177 -   Make separate safety procedure printouts and post them in your company where hazards may arise. (i.e. heavy machinery, elevators, stairwells, and breakroom)

Media and Public Relations

Every company should worry about brand. Part of branding includes sending a consistent message throughout the company. Media relations is how your company works with media outlets for the purpose of informing the general public of news relating to the company.

Public relations is how your company interacts with the public and how the public feels about your company. Public relations is influenced by your media relations and therefore both of these areas should be closely monitored.

Who is Media Authorized

In order to ensure a uniform message is sent to the media, and therefore to the public, you should first limit who is allowed to talk to the media. In this case, the media should include bloggers.

The people you choose to represent your company image should be people who share the same values and embody the spirit of the company. If the person representing your company has contrary values, you will see hesitation as well as mixed insincerity when giving the desired messages. In some cases, you may even find your media relations person giving the wrong message because it is based on her values and not the company's values. Without consciously realizing it, our personal values will be much more apparent in stressful situations, which to many people includes speaking to the public in any capacity.

The number of spokespeople should be kept small to ensure there is a uniform message. Even spouses try to keep a uniform front with their children, but as people are unique, the messages delivered tend to vary. If it is possible to have just one spokesperson, and one message, that's ideal; however, due to the nature of the wide breadth of information channels out there, it's hard to have the same person cover social media, press releases, blogs, television interviews, internal communications and other public-facing media or marketing efforts.

[ ] Step 178 -   To help media out, decide who your spokespeople will be, and include them on your website under an easily accessible media link.

Unauthorized Media Disclosures

Even with rules against it, employees will sometimes feel the need to share information with the public. They do this for any number of reasons. Sometimes, they like the feeling of having the inside knowledge, or they didn't know it was 'on the record.' It doesn't matter the reason, but what matters is how it is dealt with.

The punishment is very much reliant on the company's values and the amount of harm, if any, that was caused. You'll find that stricter companies will enforce disclosures with termination whereas more relaxed companies will discuss why the disclosure isn't beneficial to the company.

Legal Tip: If you're choosing to terminate someone, for any reason, there should be as much documentation as possible. Signed performance plans, separate agreements agreeing not to contact the media, and previous write-ups will help the employer's position if the employee files for unemployment or for wrongful termination.

Regardless of your choice for repercussion, it should be included in your employee handbook. If it is outlined in your employee handbook, it is a condition to work for the company; therefore, any punishment that doesn't violate public policy should be unquestionably enforceable.

Keep in mind that you should only be terminating (or punishing in any way) for actions that pertain to that employee's employment, or things that reflect back on the company. A blog about poodles when your employee is a software engineer would likely not reflect on the company in any way.

Legal Tip: When punishing your employees for any sort of mistake, be very careful with 'fines.' Fines are any sort of punishment that takes money away from the employee that he has already earned and is promised to him.

Media Authorization Process

To ensure that no one is confused as to her role when it comes to the media, you should outline a specific process for becoming authorized to talk to the media. This process should be outlined in the employee handbook so each employee knows what to do if she wants to talk to the media. This could include temporary authorization for a specific media communication or long term authorization for full media access. Any authorization should be in writing, so it is documented, and the writing should be included in that employee's human resources file.

Media Response

Having a set response for your employees who are approached by media is a must. The response should include a reference to who media should send inquiries to instead as well as a quick phrase to deflect the questions, such as "I'm sorry, but I'm not the person to answer your questions. All media inquiries should be directed to Mable Smith at this number 555-555-5555" would work well.

Employee Run Media

Sometimes, your employees moonlight with their own blogs and social media with large followings. In order to protect your brand and company secrets, you should make clear what can and cannot be said through outside media sources, including social media.

Things such as current projects, information on clients, internal policies, and internal conflicts within the company should never be discussed over uncontrolled media sources because these will send mixed messages about your company as well as potentially create bad public relations through negative messages.

[ ] Step 179 - Knowing what you know about media policies, add a media policy to the Workplace Expectations section of the handbook.

Leave Policies

Employees should be able to take leave for reasons outlined in your handbook, some voluntary and others are required by law.

Family Medical

Although not always required by law, it is a good idea to have some sort of medical leave for the employee and his or her close family. By giving your employees time off for illness, you actually keep them healthier by not having them stress about what will happen in case of an emergency.

If you have more than 50 employees, you have additional rules under the Family Medical Leave Act that affect the leave you must provide to your employees.

[ ] Step 180 - Review the Family and Medical Leave portion of the handbook and make any necessary changes to reflect your policies.

[ ] Step 181 - Obtain the poster mentioned in the Family and Medical Leave portion of the sample handbook and add that to your employment folder on your computer.

Jury Duty

By law, you're required to give time off for your employee when she needs to perform her civic duty of jury duty. You should include this in your employee handbook because you will create goodwill with your employees when you showcase their rights under the law. If it isn't listed, your employees may believe that they'll get in trouble for attempting to take time off for jury duty.

Some companies actually give extra bonuses for performing this civic duty. If it fits with your values, you may want to incentive your employees to not try to get out of jury duty through perks and recognition.

> [ ] Step 182 - Review the Jury Duty portion of the handbook and make any changes that fit your company's values.

Military Leave

Many times, you will have employees that are in the military, especially the Reserves. These employees will have to take time off to go to training or in case they get deployed. By law, you are required to give your military servicemen and women time off when they are required to for their training or deployment.

If it fits with your values, you may want to consider giving special thanks to these members.

> [ ] Step 183 - Review the Military Leave portion of the handbook and make any changes you see fit.

Court Cases

Sometimes, your employees need to sue or get sued for various reasons, and other times, they're witnesses to a crime or in a civil case. It's important to note that many times, having to appear in court is not because of something the person intended to do. Therefore, when your employees have to appear in court, you should have some mechanism to handle this.

Sometimes, your employee is required to use his paid time off and other times, he is given a few special days for circumstances like these. You'll want to craft a policy that makes sense with your company values and list it in the employee handbook. Having a set policy that is uniformly upheld will make your employees far more comfortable when these circumstances come up. If the employee is subpoenaed, you may be required under state law to give that employee time off without deducting vacation time.

> [ ] Step 184 - If you want it, add a leave policy to your handbook regarding court cases.

Legal Tip: If the employee has to go to court for the company, this isn't time off, but rather working for the company.

Voting

Everyone needs the ability to vote. If you want to make sure your employees do not need to stand in incredibly long lines, you may want to consider giving additional time off or changed schedules for days when there is voting taking place in your locality. Historically, the voting places are most busy over lunch break and the hours right before they close. If you give your employees the option to vote in the morning or early afternoon, they will have much shorter wait times.

It's up to you how to handle voting. Typically, not everyone can be absent from your business for half a day, so you may want to give a staggered time off, or just allow people to use their paid time off to cover their voting. This is an area that is completely values-driven, but should still be listed in your employee handbook so your employees will know how to handle voting.

[ ] Step 185 -   Review the Election section of the handbook and make any changes you see necessary.

Sickness

Employees get sick. This is bound to happen. How you deal with it is up to you; however, sickness, if spread throughout a company, can create massive losses in revenue. Your sickness policies should be relaxed enough to encourage those who are sick to stay home, yet strict enough to discourage abuse by your employees when they are not sick.

Forcing employees to use their paid time off when they are sick is generally a bad idea because they'll just show up to work sick and infect everyone around them, whereas allowing employees off whenever they want may not be a good strategy if there aren't mechanisms in place to still ensure the work gets done. The use of bonuses for productivity has been fairly successful for incentivizing employees to continue to get their work done.

As with every policy, make sure that it fits with your values.

[ ] Step 186 -   Review the Sick Leave policy in the handbook and make any changes that reflect your company's policies.

Vacation

A week of vacation every year is worth a lot more to an employee than the equivalent in money he would have earned during that time. When seeking out the better employees, you will need vacation policies to entice them to join your team. Furthermore, vacation helps rejuvenate your employees so they perform better when they come back. Vacation time is a win for both you and the employee, so there is very little reason not to offer vacation time, or paid time off.

It is up to you to determine what the optimal amount of paid time off is and how your employees can use it. For example, are your employees allowed to accumulate the time between years and then take a 30-week vacation? Additionally, are your employees allowed to take vacation with limited notice or do they need to give at least a couple weeks' advance notice? What about vacation time over holidays? Is vacation time on a first-come, first-served basis or based on some form of seniority?

[ ] Step 187 -   Review the vacation policy in the handbook and make changes to reflect your policy.

Legal Tip: In many states, accrued vacation time is owed to the employee if the employee is terminated. Check to see your state's policies on accrued vacation time.

Bereavement

When family and friends pass away, we all want to be there to say our words and support the immediate family in their time of need. We mostly do this for our own benefit - to give us peace of mind and have closure. Without this closure, we end up restless and uneasy, searching for some other way to gain closure. This uneasiness causes a lot of distraction in the workplace. Therefore employers like yourself should give the necessary time off for a person to mourn their loved ones.

The questions lie in how much time off is appropriate and who this bereavement time off is allowed for. Does it qualify if your sister's husband's aunt passed away? What level of separation is this policy limited to and is it based on familial degrees or on closeness of the person? Do friends count? These are all questions you will need to answer while crafting your policy. Some states require that the employee be able to take time off without repercussion from the employer.

[ ] Step 188 -   Review the bereavement leave policy and make any changes that fit your policy.

ADA Compliance

Under the Americans With Disabilities Act (ADA), an employer is required to make reasonable accommodations for their employee who suffers from a disability that impairs a major life function. For example, a Deaf employee may require closed captioning on training videos if you do not already have them.

This is an area that can be fairly expansive, but you will find that most accommodations are fairly simple corrections that may even improve operations for everyone at the company. When the necessary accommodations are not affordable, there is an exception for undue burden on the employer.

Tip: There are some tax credits available for making accommodations. Credits are far more beneficial than deductions, so take advantage of these.

This is an area you will have to address on a case-by-case basis because you will not be sure what accommodations you will need to make until they actually present themselves.

Tip: Discriminations against persons with disabilities is illegal. It is also unwise because a disability likely does not mean a person cannot do the job they're applying for. Discrimination in any form hurts your company because you eliminate potential candidates without reason.

Holidays

On which days do you close your business? Are your holidays based on the religion and nationality of yourself or do you give holiday time off for your employees of other faiths and nationalities? Holidays can be very important to people or not at all. It's an important area to consider when determining when an employee can take off for holidays.

Furthermore, is everyone allowed to take off, or is there a mechanism to ensure that certain people are still working on these holidays? For example, hospitals need to stay open so a certain percent of the staff will still be working on holidays like Christmas. "Floating holidays" can be a great way to handle other religions and nationalities, allowing your employees a certain number of holidays throughout the year that don't have to fall on any specific holidays.

[ ] Step 189 -   Review the Holiday Pay section of the employee handbook, and make any changes necessary. You may need to rename it if you're closed on specific holidays instead of offering extra pay.

Reimbursement for Training

In a lot of fields, the employees must be trained prior to beginning work. In some of these cases, the training is formal and through third parties. Take the software industry, for example. In order to create uniform products following a particular set of rules, the software developers may all need to go through a specific training on the software product they will be using. This training can cost thousands of dollars and is therefore quite the investment by the company.

Some companies feel the need to require that the employee reimburse the company if she leaves the company within a certain period of time after receiving the training. If this is something you will need to protect yourself, this can be written into the employee handbook and employee contract.

[ ] Step 190 -   If you want this to be included, you must include it in your handbook; however, be careful when reimbursement drops your employee's wages to below minimum wage.

Intellectual Property and Confidentiality (NDA)

Your intellectual property and your trade secrets can be some of the most valuable assets of your company. In order to protect them, you will want a policy on the books regarding what an employee is and is not allowed to discuss with third parties. This is called a nondisclosure agreement and should be a separate document signed by your employees when they start their employment. It should, however, also be included in the employee handbook to ensure that the employee knows that this is a condition of his employment.

[ ] Step 191 -   If a nondisclosure agreement makes sense for your company, include this in your handbook, but also have employees sign a separate, more thorough, NDA when they begin work as well as all the other documents you are having them sign.

Non-Competition Agreements

Non-competition agreements (sometimes referred to as restrictive covenants against competition) vary wildly between states. Some states do not allow non-competition agreements at all in employment settings, while others are fairly relaxed about them.

The ones that do permit them generally require them to be in writing, part of an employment agreement, based on consideration (value), limited as to time and territory, and not in violation of public policy. How each of these criteria are interpreted is up to the individual state courts, and there are many nuances as well.

[ ] Step 192 - If this is something you want in your employment agreements or handbook, you should consult a business or employment attorney in your state who is familiar with these agreements.

Tip: In many states, non-competes that are poorly written are simply not enforced. Therefore, this is an area that, if important, should be handled by an attorney.

CHAPTER 17 - STANDARD OPERATING PROCEDURE

Successful companies are nothing more than a set of systems that can run almost irrespective of who is running them, as long as that person has the necessary skills to do so. The systems need to be uniform so that the next cog in the system, or the customer, knows exactly what the output of the previous system will be.

Imagine that every system in your company is a piece of manufacturing machinery. The piece of machinery takes inputs and delivers an output or outputs of a basically uniform nature. When the outputs are not uniform, they are considered mistakes or duds in the manufacturing line. The next system cannot use them, or if the next system in line is sales, the customer wouldn't want them because the outputs are not what the customer expected.

In the same way, your systems need to be uniform. If multiple people in your company need to work on the overall process, each part needs to be uniform so that the other people will know exactly what to expect and what is expected of them. Your ultimate outputs need to be uniform too so that your customers know what to expect of you. Any uncertainty in product will hurt your brand. In business, nobody likes uncertainty.

Obviously, creative endeavors are harder to make uniform; however, the level of quality should still be uniform. If you have systems in place to ensure that you're still providing a quality product to your customers, you'll be able to keep it as uniform as possible.

Write Everything Down

In order to make sure everything is uniform, write it down from the very first time you run through the process. This is called your standard operating procedure, or SOP for short. It should be detailed enough that if you quit your business, someone who has the same skills as you can come in and run the business with minimal delay. The checklist is the basic form of system control mechanism, but you will more likely than not need decision trees, also known as mind maps. A sample decision tree is shown below:

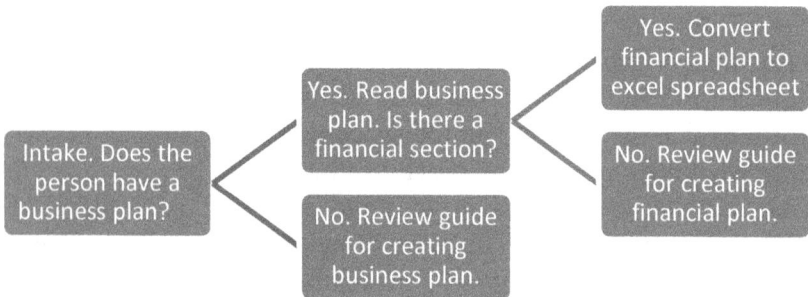

```
Intake. Does the                Yes. Read business          Yes. Convert
person have a                   plan. Is there a            financial plan to
business plan?                  financial section?          excel spreadsheet

                                No. Review guide            No. Review guide
                                for creating                for creating
                                business plan.              financial plan.
```

These trees can reference other trees or be all in one. They're able to be handwritten or typed up. There are many programs that are specifically designed for creating mind maps and decision trees. The object is to find the one that you think best conveys your systems. You can even create computer programs to do exactly what these do without leaving much input to the user.

Ideally, your systems will be simple enough that anyone can read and comprehend them. If you have to explain a part of the guide, it isn't complete. Therefore, you should include explanations for the portions you had to explain on an ongoing basis.

When your systems change, you should change them in the guide first. The reason for this is that once you change the system and start implementing it, you will no longer think of the change, and therefore won't think of the system guide until an issue comes up.

[ ] Step 193 -   Take any systems or procedures you've written previously in this book and include them in your SOP. Specifically look at Chapter 11 for processes already made.

Tip: Use tabs, headings, or other mechanisms for organization to keep your SOP as organized as possible. If you need help, hire someone who is organized to help put this together for you.

Institutional Memory

Tip: You're not going to be doing every task in your company forever. Keep that in mind as you grow.

One of the major advantages of having everything written down is the ability to easily pass off responsibilities. You can control every aspect of the new employee without having to micromanage everything. This eliminates waste and increases uniformity, which in turn, makes you money.

Almost every entrepreneur works in every section of the company at some point. Most entrepreneurs also do not desire to continue working in every section of the company for the rest of their lives. For example, an entrepreneur, in the beginning, is the sales person, the producer, the administrative staff and the CEO. Let's say her first hire is a sales person.

When she hires the sales person, she can either spend months going over every scenario with the new hire and then supervise strictly to ensure things are working out, or she can have a guide already set up for the new hire to follow. Training, without the guide, relies on the business owner remembering every aspect of the sales process. This isn't possible. It is also not possible to write everything down, but you will have a vastly larger percentage if you are dedicated to keeping good records.

If you write the missed instructions as you train the first hire, you will also have a great guide for the second hire and a more uniform training program in place.

> [ ] Step 194 -   List all the transactions you've already completed as part of your company and the steps to complete them in appropriate sections of your SOP.

Guidelines

The Standard Operating Procedure is the 'how' of your company. It outlines how everything gets accomplished. The processes you develop above should be included in here, but the SOP should also contain the company rules and guidelines. What follows are many different possible things to include in your SOP. If it doesn't apply in your situation, skip it.

Meeting Conduct

Included in the Standard Operating Procedure is how meetings are conducted. Meetings should have standard rules, and these rules should be clearly outlined so that everyone can understand what their roles are in the meeting. Without clear expectations, meetings would be less productive and would create a lot of wasted time. In more creative meetings, like brainstorming, be sure to not be so structured to the point where you are stifling creativity.

The Standard Operating Procedure should include who is in charge of any meeting, or how the leader of the meeting is determined. Without a leader, there is virtually no structure; therefore, a leader is the cornerstone of a meeting. The leader will control who gets to talk, when motions are heard, and what rules of order are used, as well as any other specific rules that a company would like to see. Leaders, of course, would have the right to delegate these powers, unless the rules state otherwise.

Your SOP should also include where meetings are conducted. Many companies have a boardroom, but if your company is small, you may not have adequate meeting space for some meetings. There shouldn't be time wasted trying to arrange places to meet. Instead, these places should already be discovered and listed in the standard operating procedure.

Meetings can sometimes be conducted over electronic communication, like Voice over IP and video conferencing. Your operating procedure should include if these are allowed and what programs are allowed. Having one or two specific pieces of software will eliminate confusion and allow the program work smoothly. Meetings can be ruined by technical difficulties, so finding and choosing the best software for your company is important, should you choose to have meetings electronically.

> [ ] Step 195 -   Create a section in your Standard Operating Procedure that describes what types of meetings there are, how the meetings are conducted, what software will be used (if any), and any other rules that may apply.

Interview Conduct

We went over how interviews should be conducted earlier in the Building the Team section. From that, you should have an idea how you want to conduct your interviews.

> [ ] Step 196 -   Create a section and include your rules and questions for interviewing candidates of various levels in your organization.

Tip: Eventually, you won't be the person conducting interviews. Create this portion as though you gave up that role tomorrow and still have top of the line candidates.

Sales Scripts

Some people would argue that sales is an art form, and although they may well be correct, by stating that sales is an art form, people are arguing that you cannot standardize it. This is not true. If you've ever been to a structured networking event, you've heard similar sales scripts recited time after time. Similarly, those annoying phone conversations from telemarketers all have the same elements because they're sales scripts.

Without even realizing it, you typically give some sort of structure to every salesperson. When you say "emphasize" this or "don't say that" to your salesperson, you are giving some level of standardization and taking away from the creativity. Just by having a standard product, you're already limiting the person's creativity, so it shouldn't be a surprise that you should put a significant amount of controls on that salesperson's job. Any of these controls should be written down.

Sales scripts should emphasize your company values, what sets your company apart, the underlying intrinsic value that you are selling, and the opportunity cost of getting such a product or service. These are the four things that every consumer really wants to know.

You should put limitations on your salesperson when protecting your brand. Salespeople are the face of your company and directly impact your brand each and every day.

You should also put limitations on your salesperson for legal reasons. Sometimes, there are things you can and cannot say when selling your product or service. For example, lawyers in certain states cannot use the word "specialize" unless they are a board recognized specialist. If a salesperson flaunted that his boss was an attorney who specialized in bankruptcy when she really didn't, that attorney could be in a lot of trouble through the state bar.

> [ ] Step 197 -   Create a section called sales and include the various sales rules, guidelines, and scripts you want your salespeople to use. Be sure to include any do's and don'ts of the job.

Service Procedures

If you're in a service industry, or a part of what you do involves a service or act to provide the product, then you want to describe in great detail the step-by-step procedure to that particular service. For example, if you need to install a camera inside of a store when you sell the camera, you should create a guide for your current and future installation people about how to position the camera, what to avoid, what screws to use or screwless mounts, and any other details a service person would need to know if they've never installed a camera before.

This goes back into uniform delivery of a product and service and directly impacts your brand. It also eliminates waste because you've detailed out a procedure that works. Any deviation from that procedure might cause the serviceman to take longer or be forced to fix the problem they've created.

Anytime that a better procedure is discovered, it should be noted and a decision should be made whether or not to implement the new procedure. The cost of doing so should be weighed against the benefits of doing so. If it is more beneficial to implement the new procedure, it should be done and reflected in the guide. All people currently using that guide or performing that service should be retrained to do it the new way in order to keep things uniform.

[ ] Step 198 -   Create a section in your SOP that outlines the rules, guidelines, principles, and everything you want your servicepersons to follow regarding providing your service.

Product Guidelines

If you sell a product, your standard operating procedure should include every detail about that product, excluding only those things that you intend to keep secret. The secret things should still be written down, but in another place and locked away. Definitely keep them in a fireproof and waterproof safe or backed up on several password-protected servers.

Your product guidelines should include all details required to manufacture or create the product as well as processes necessary to maintain and store the product if there are special instructions to do so.

Your product plans should include the details and specifications that are required to be able to recreate the manufacturing guidelines should that need be done. For a lot of products, these designs are done through some engineering program, but this varies wildly depending on the industry and what type of product it is. Obviously, a pharmaceutical drug is very different from a beer can in process and product plans.

As with everything in your standard operating procedure, these should be incredibly detailed so that anyone with the necessary skill could come in and recreate or run your business from these plans.

[ ] Step 199 -   Create your product guidelines/plans section of your Standard Operating Procedure.

Tip: This will likely be the longest portion of your SOP, as it is the core aspect of your business.

Call Scripts

If your business model includes calling people or receiving calls, it may be wise to create call scripts. These scripts could be for cold calling, follow up calls, special requests, or anything else that requires a phone that occurs regularly to the same or different people.

A sample follow up call could go something like this: "Good [morning/afternoon/evening] [Mr./Mrs./Miss] [LAST NAME], it was a pleasure seeing you on [DATE MET] at [LOCATION MET] regarding your upcoming wedding. I greatly value your willingness to take the time to sit down with me, and I want you to know that we will be dedicated toward making your wedding a day to remember. We hope you took the time to review the materials we provided you and would like to know if you have any questions at this time."

Cold call scripts and special requests are so specific to the nature of the call that it would be difficult to give an example without knowing the details surrounding the product or service and the reason for the specific call. They should, however, all take into account the company's values and brand as well as the intrinsic need that the company is seeking to fulfill.

[ ] Step 200 -   Create a section, or include in the various sections, any call scripts you want your staff to follow. This is different than sales scripts and can be a part of any portion of your company.

Important Community Connections

Any time your company relies on other companies or people, the contacts should be recorded in the standard operating procedure and changed as the contact person changes. This eliminates the possibility of one employee or partner hording all the connections that are needed to make a company run.

Take, for example, a government contracting company. This company likely has connections in the government agencies they work for and should always have these connections written down for easy reference in case of questions or when looking for new work.

It may be cliché, but you should also have your state, local and national representatives in this standard operating procedure, updated as they change from year to year. You should keep in touch with at least a few of them to ensure your business is adequately represented in the legislative branch of the government. This doesn't mean you should lobby or flood your representative with emails, but you should be on his or her radar.

[ ] Step 201 -   Create your Community Connections section of your SOP. Be sure to include any media or political connections you might have.

List of Company Contacts

When you work with other companies, you want to keep track of their connections as well. This will actually be very similar to how you keep track of your networking connections, but instead of individuals, you'd be keeping track of partner companies. Many companies have business relationships with other companies in order to better serve their customers, so whenever you need to contact the partner company, you will need to know how to get in touch with them.

A Customer Relations Management tool (CRM) or Network Relationship Management tool (NRM) is a piece of software that helps keep track of those connections you, or your company, has. A CRM tool focuses on sales whereas an NRM tool focuses on helping those within your network. The two can be used together, but usually a business will fit better with one or the other.

[ ] Step 202 - Create a section that outlines your company connections or the place where you store them. Many people use a CRM or NRM tool to do this for them.

Tip: Use MyNetworkingBuddy.com (an NRM) to store your company contacts, as it is a useful way to do value-added networking with significantly less effort.

Training Procedure

If you're planning on growing, you'll likely be training people. When you're training people, you want to have the best training possible, with the least waste possible. Uniform training procedures lead to uniform production which leads to a more successful business.

Hopefully, you will not be the person training each and every new hire. Once you get the training procedures written down, you have other people follow it in a uniform way. Having any discrepancies gives some individuals the feeling that others are receiving preferential treatment, which leads to unhappiness and mistrust.

Part of training should be reviewing the parts of the standard operating procedure that pertain to the new hire. If it is done right, the person will not need much additional training beyond that.

[ ] Step 203 - Yes, create a portion of your SOP for how to train someone using this SOP. It will never be 100% intuitive, so it is important to have instructions on how to train someone here as well.

Board Procedures

If you have a board of directors or a board of trustees, advisors, or anything else, you will want procedures that are specific to the board to be in the standard operating procedure. A lot of what will be included in this portion will be regarding how meetings are conducted. It is likely that meetings with the board will be very different from meetings that occur regularly in the business;

therefore, different rules should be outlined to ensure that these important people will not have to waste as much time.

Selection of board members, mechanisms for contacting board members, board members' contact information and any other rules that pertain to the board members should be included in here. Keep in mind that nothing in these procedures can overrule your articles of incorporation or bylaws/operating agreement unless the bylaws and operating agreement allow for them to be overridden by the standard operating procedure.

[ ] Step 204 -   Any procedures that are not listed in the Meetings portion of the SOP or the company's governing document should be listed in the SOP. You've already addressed many of these things if you went through the Building the Team portion.

Software

Most every company now uses software of some sort. In order to ensure compatibility, any software that is used should be listed and described in the standard operating procedure. This description should include what the software is, where to get it, how to use it and what it will be used for in the company. It should also include the minimum system requirements, if any, that the software has in order to be used. This is all good information to help others get acquainted with that software.

If you have someone who is in charge of information technology (IT) for the company, he should be the one to draft this portion of the guide and his contact information should be at the beginning of this section. If it is a separate business that is in charge of the IT for your company, that business's contact information should be listed at the top of this section along with any information about a contact person at that IT business and should be updated whenever there are changes.

[ ] Step 205 -   Create a section on technology. This can be a larger section because you need to define meeting software, word processing, accounting, billing, time keeping, and more in your business.

Instructions

Finally, anything else that needs instructions or explanation should be in the SOP. If you find yourself explaining something to someone else, it should be in the SOP, in as detailed a way as possible. If one person had the question, sometime later, another person likely will too.

[ ] Step 206 -   If you can think of anything else, record that in the SOP as well.

A more detailed Standard Operating Procedure makes your company more valuable because it is more efficient and easier to grow and scale. Your SOP is an asset of your company.

Documentation of the Process

Everything you do in the creation of the product or the running of your company should be documented. Your goal should be to document clearly enough that anyone with the necessary skillsets could come in and take over any portion of the company. This will not only add value to your company, but it will allow you to clear up mental energy for the development of your company instead of the product.

Documentation frees you from having to develop the same process twice. If it's already documented in a way that you can easily access it, you will not need to worry about wasted energy later on when you need to revisit the process. Instead of starting from scratch, you'll have your previously determined optimal way of producing the uniform product.

Tip: You'll never completely avoid memorizing things. If you do the same task over and over again, you likely will not want to refer to the SOP each time, but you should only keep those tasks in your head that are frequent enough to make memorization efficient.

CHAPTER 18 - RECORD KEEPING

"Cleanliness is next to Godliness." – John Wesley

Good records make for a good company. They add value in case you want to sell, decrease confusion when it comes to disagreements, decrease the learning curve for new employees and managers, and document the life of the company so you can see the clear direction the company is heading in.

Decisions, and the Record

The written record of processes is also great in case you come across a difficult situation you discovered before. If you put how you addressed it last time, you will not need to worry about expending large amounts of mental energy and time coming to a similar conclusion. This will also keep your decisions uniform so your employees, vendors, customers or other people who work with you will not feel that you are being unfair or picking favorites. This uniformity in decision making will brand you as more stable and more predictable. Therefore, you will be seen as fair and easier to work with.

You also want to record any business decisions you made. If you decided to focus heavily on a particular line of product for three months, write it down. It can always change, but you want to keep a record of the decisions you've made and why you made the decision.

Meeting Minutes

In any meeting with someone who makes an impact on your

business or some joint venture, you should record the discussions and the decisions in minute form. In many meetings, if your company is a corporation, these may be required by law, but even if they're not required, they're a great idea.

The worst thing for any business relationship is loss of trust, and in the case of differing thoughts about decisions in a meeting, trust tends to be lost. If you thought a decision was made in one way and your partner thought it was made in another way, then there's going to be a disagreement, even if it's just a small one. Disagreements can lead to mistrust, but if you have the meeting and immediately follow up with the decisions presented in a clear way to your partner, any decision can be settled quickly and without the loss of trust.

The sooner the minutes are presented to your partner, the better. Ideally, they are written up during the meeting and presented to your partner by the end for approval. That way, no one leaves without being certain which decisions were made.

If, months later, the decision is questioned, you will have a documented reference of the decision and the details surrounding it.

Your meeting minutes should include who was present, date and time that the meeting started, any items discussed with positions taken on each item, and any decisions made or action items required. More detail is better because it will clear up any ambiguity at a later date.

Tip: Meeting minutes do not need to be pretty, nor do they need to be complex. The best minutes are clear and contain a list of action items to be completed.

Your process guide, written decisions, and meeting minutes should be comprehensive enough that in the event you pass away or leave the company, the company should be able to continue with minimal setback. Of course, if you're deceased, you may not care as much about this. Your family or any third party may not know how to run your company. You wouldn't want to leave them in the position where they have this valuable asset that they cannot use in any meaningful way.

Tip: Great processes and institutional memory increases the value of your business.

[ ] Step 207 -   Create some sort of system for documenting your business decisions, minutes, and other important business information. This can be on paper or computerized, but computers are generally preferred so you can update it or have backups.

Tip: Many lawsuits can be avoided by having excellent records. They help keep you organized and also give you a stronger position if someone challenges you at a later date.

CHAPTER 19 - PROTECTIONS & INTELLECTUAL PROPERTY

Every business needs some form of protection. Many of these are built in, like the idea of ownership in our marketplace. For the protections that are not built in, you will need to address them so that you don't have to worry about someone stealing your idea or your business.

Intellectual Property

Protecting yourself is a huge concern, especially with intellectual property. Whether you're protecting your business concept, your new piece of technology, your slogan or even the words you use in your advertising, you should visit the methods of protecting your property from the hands of others.

Black's Law Dictionary defines intellectual property as "a category of intangible rights protecting commercially valuable products of the human intellect." This includes copyrights, trademarks, patents, and trade secrets.

"Property is a bundle of sticks" – Every Law School

Trademark

A trademark protects words, phrases, symbols, designs or some combination thereof that signifies and distinguishes the company, or source of the good, from another. The trademark can apply to the company as a whole or just a subset of it, product line or an individual product itself.

A service mark is the same as a trademark except that it applies to a service oppose to a good. Trade dress can also be trademarked, and it includes things such as the interior of a restaurant or the decorative look of the outside of a building. This is an important area, especially if you intend to franchise your business. For example, look at every Outback Steakhouse.

Why would you want a trademark or service mark? Having this mark in your pocket helps protect your identity, and in some cases, really protects your entire business idea if it's based on a marketing or branding idea.

Protection of this mark will protect your brand, which in many companies, is more crucial than any other types of intellectual property. The main test for trademark infringement is whether the other company or product will likely be confused for yours, thereby diluting your brand value.

Look at Puffs facial tissues. If any other company was allowed to label their product as "Puffs" facial tissues, it would ruin Puff's brand and their company as a whole. People buy Puffs because they've built up trust in the product. Without that trust, no one would pay the extra money because they would be unsure whether they're receiving the soft, yet durable, facial tissue that neither chafes nor crumbles or if they'll receive the generic scratchy tissues that couldn't hold up to half a hamster sneeze.

This is only one of the areas you should consider protecting, and it is relatively simple to do so.

[ ] Step 208 -   Write down a list of trademarks, or service marks, you would be interested in getting protected.

[ ] Step 209 -   Go through your list from the previous step and ask yourself if your company would be harmed by someone else using that mark?

[ ] Step 210 -   If the answer for any of your marks was 'yes' in the previous step, you should run a search on the mark on the USPTO website to see if your mark is available for registration.

Note: We could write a whole book on how to run a trademark search. There are a lot of resources available, but if you're serious about registering, you should speak to an attorney. Attempting to register a mark that conflicts with someone else is expensive and can lead to you getting sued.

Copyright

Copyrights are your way of protecting your exclusive rights to reproduce, distribute, perform, display, and/or adapt your original work into what is called a derivative. Whenever you create something, you automatically have an all rights reserved copyright on the content. This is an automatic right that belongs exclusively to you once you create something creative. The copyright is on the content, not the idea or the name. If you write a book, the creative content of the book is copyrighted.

Imagine each work or image as a building block. Also, each quote or protected content from someone else is a building block as well. Once you've assembled enough of these building blocks together to create something that no one else has made, you've created something that automatically has a copyright on it. There is, unfortunately, no set formula for determining when something is enough to have a copyright. For example, titles of books are typically not copyrighted because they're not unique enough.

If you're using someone else's content, then you're unable to copyright that content because that other person already has a copyright on it. You may be allowed to use it, however, because of the principle of Fair Use, derivatives, or through the use of proper citations. Describing what Fair Use is would take a book in itself. The short version is that certain amounts of a person's copyrighted material may be used without the owner's permission as long as it doesn't materially affect the marketability of the copyrighted material and the use of the copyrighted material fits within specific categories of use.

A registered copyright comes with the presumption you created it first, along with statutory damages and attorney fees. The registered copyright is very useful when you're attempting to enforce your copyright because of these things.

Tip: Unless your product is creative in nature, you likely will not want to register your copyrighted works.

[ ] Step 211 -   Go through your creative products and ask (1) is this work something I will continue to make money off of and (2) will I lose any money if someone copies my work?

[ ] Step 212 -   If you answered yes to both of the above questions for any product, you should look into registering the copyright. You can do this process yourself fairly simply, but if you want professional help, you can consult with an intellectual property attorney.

Author's Note: On any works I think will be reused, and any work I intend to profit off of, I choose to file for a registered copyright. The process is simple and the cost is low.

Patent

Patents are the strongest of the intellectual property protections, and sometimes, they are the most valuable part of a startup business. Patents can be obtained on a wide variety of new products or processes. If your product or process is unique, you may want to consider whether a patent would be right for you.

You can patent a process, a machine, an article of manufacture, a composition of matter or any new and useful improvement of any of these. Useful is loosely defined, so as long as you can come up with a use, you qualify for that requirement. There are some other requirements, though. Your idea or innovation must also be novel, not obvious, and clearly explained and documented so that someone equally skilled could make and use the invention.

Some people find satisfaction in going through the patent process themselves, but most people will need the help of a patent attorney, at some point. Patent attorneys are a subset of attorneys. Whereas, an attorney can normally help with any issue that comes up, this is not the case when it comes to patents. Only patents attorneys are licensed to help you with your patent prosecution (creation and filing of the patent) or prior art search.

A prior art search is the process of ensuring that there is no other patent out there that you're infringing upon. Prior art searches usually include a global element, and only a patent attorney will know the applicable rules and procedures if someone in another company has patented, or is in the process of patenting, a similar product or process.

With a patent attorney, this process will cost tens of thousands of dollars, so you should be prepared for this cost. Because of the cost, and because you almost certainly need an attorney to do this right, you should ensure you have the right one for the job. Feel free to discuss with several attorneys prior to selecting one, and try to avoid any that charge a consultation fee unless they are highly recommended by someone you trust.

Author's note: It is this author's opinion that consultation fees should not be charged by attorneys, or any industry, without the consultation offering significant value. They're a method of taking money from clients without any promise of value. I've seen several people sit down for a consultation to be told that the attorney could not help that person, yet still charge them in excess of $500.

Having a patent gives you the exclusive right to make and sell, or even use, your invention for 20 years. This gives you the option to create a business around the product, license the product, or just sit on the idea without allowing anyone else to use it. Depending on your invention, any of these options may be the correct one.

> [ ] Step 213 -   If you have a patentable idea, you should speak with a patent attorney.

Patent attorneys are specialized attorneys who have passed the patent bar exam. An attorney who has not passed the patent bar exam cannot give you advice on patents and should not because we do not know enough about them to give proper advice.

Contracts

It's a common misconception that contracts have to be in writing. In fact, every time you exchange one thing of value for another thing of value or money, you have created a contract. The contract can be in writing, verbal or nonverbal such as gesturing. Contracts may either be expressed, as they would be in writing or verbally, or they can be implied. Implied contracts arise if there are terms of an agreement that are just understood, meaning they were never discussed.

For example, if you've had the same company mow your lawn year after year and that company comes to mow your lawn after the first sign of growth in the spring, you likely will have an implied contract because it is just assumed they will show up again to mow your lawn this season. That's your understanding. Implied contracts happen a lot when there was an understanding or in long term relationships.

So, how does a contract protect you? It protects you from the unknown. Few things are more hazardous to a relationship than mismatched expectations. Contracts are there to ensure that everyone is on the same page. Without these, courts will be forced to interpret how they think the parties would have decided this agreement based on the facts surrounding the agreement. This can cost a lot of money and legal fees should the contract have to go to court. Business owners will typically negotiate themselves into a lower position at trial than they would have had with a well written contract in place.

If you have the contract clearly laid out, there won't be any loss in negotiation because you know how strong the position is, regardless of what the position is. The other party will like this as well because he won't have to expend the time and effort trying to negotiate, or go to court.

Furthermore, uncertainty is a huge source of stress in everyone's lives. Clear contracts eliminate much of this unnecessary uncertainty, and that is why "legalese" contracts likely aren't the best for most small businesses.

It is a common misconception that contracts have to be written in legalese. As many law schools are now teaching, this legalese is counterproductive to the business process. (Why we need schools to teach us that unreadable contracts slow things down, I don't know.) Many lawyers and legal scholars will argue that contracts written in plain English are actually better for business and lead to fewer conflicts, clearer expectations, and less stress. A contract that one or more parties did not understand before entering into the contract creates the same level of uncertainty and conflict as having no written contract at all.

The defense "that's not what I thought I was signing" actually works from time to time. It's called fraud, and it can create more headaches for the drafting party than just breach of contract or unclear expectations in terms of both legal consequences as well as branding consequences. No one wants to work with someone or sign an agreement with someone who is known for confusing contracts or unfair dealings.

Plain English contracts contain all of the key terms you'd see in any contract: price, duration, work performed, products sold, method of payment, etc., as well as anything that the parties found important. Instead of putting these details into unreadable jargon, they're put in the party's own language so that they both agree that the words convey exactly what they meant. There's something lost in the translation if a lawyer wrote it and interpreted it.

[ ] Step 214 -   For any of your products or services, either hire an attorney or create your own contract by listing the ten most important criteria for the relationship. This should include price, parties, signature lines, duration, termination provisions, and dispute resolution. Anything else that is important to you should also be included.

Tip: The most problems happen with contracts when one party tries to be too clever. This leads to ambiguity and misinterpretation.

Tip: It is only when there is a problem that contracts make a difference. If there's no problem, no one reads the contract.

License Agreements

If you've made an invention or creative content, you will want license agreements to set up who can use your invention or content and how they are allowed to use it. License agreements may also work the other way when you want to use some intellectual property of another person or company. To ensure that you're not accidentally stealing it, you will want the terms of your permission to be in writing. This is called a license because it doesn't give you ownership, but rather permission to use. Just like a driver's license is a permission to drive, a license to use text from a book is permission to use that text.

Licenses can be as open or as restrictive as needed. A license can read something like this: "I give John Doe a license to use my work in *John Doe, the Biography* for whatever purpose he desires." This is obviously one of the least restrictive licenses because it gives him a license to use the content for "whatever purpose he desires."

Other times, you will see licenses that are more restrictive, like the following example:

"I grant Jamie Doe a non-exclusive, non-transferrable, license to use the sixty second clip from Vampires, the Girl Next Door starting at thirty-six minutes and three seconds only for the educational purpose of including such clip in the PowerPoint slide to be shown on February 15, 2014 at Greenacre Community College in Jamie Doe's psychology classroom. This license will expire on February 16, 2014 and can be revoked at any time by myself."

This one is a license for a very specific purpose and gives the recipient very little leeway. Restrictive licenses are very common, especially when it comes to copyrights.

It wouldn't be the legal field if there weren't exceptions to the rule. Although Copyrights, Trademarks, and Patents give the owners of those pieces of intellectual property a lot of control, exceptions such as Fair Use can give other people a lot of leeway. The example above would likely fit into the Fair Use Exception.

> [ ] Step 215 -   Make your license agreement the same way you made your contracts. Either hire an attorney or list the ten most important considerations, taking what you know from above.

Leases

The major difference between a lease and a license is what you are getting. A lease is an ownership interest, meaning you actually own and may act as the owner of such property, whereas a license is only the right to use. You can get a license of a piece of real property, but that only gives you the right to use it. Your use could be living there, but the original owner retains full rights to use the property as well. In a lease, you have the exclusive right to possess and control the property, unless otherwise specified. You also have the right to exclude others. In a license, you do not have that right, unless it is bargained for as well.

With tangible property, you typically see leases more than you see licenses. Take, for example, a piece of farm equipment. If you need it for a certain period of time, you'd lease that property for that time.

Leases contain a myriad of different terms depending on the circumstances. A lease for a piece of farm equipment is going to be vastly different than a lease for office space. What you will always see is price, parties involved, length of the lease and the lessee's rights when possessing the property.

Many times, you will see restrictions on usage of the property as well as a security deposit to protect the lessor. Most things in any lease are put there to protect the rights of the lessor and the property itself.

Whenever you're signing a large lease (one that will greatly affect your business), you should negotiate the lease. If your lessor is unwilling to negotiate, you should find someone who is willing to negotiate. In leases, you should never waive your rights to sue or agree to pay if you're unable to take possession on the start date. You should never agree to allow the lessor unlimited access to the property, nor allow them to disclaim all rights and responsibilities. There are a lot of other red flags in leases. If it seems like trouble, it likely is. If you need help understanding your rights, you should seek the help of an attorney familiar with leases.

One of the favorite provisions that lessors try to sneak past lessees is the waiver to the right of notice upon eviction or repossession. This means that you waive your right to receive notice that you're being sued and therefore, you won't show up and defend yourself. Although it is typically not an issue, the few times it is leaves a business owner feeling blindsided when the sheriff shows up.

Attorneys who think that they're clever put all of these things in leases, but all that really happened was that attorneys preyed on the fact that few people read the lease closely and even fewer people try to negotiate. Now that there are a lot of people negotiating these leases, you will find more and more lessors willing to negotiate or just start out with friendlier terms.

In many different types of leases, there are laws revolving around what can and cannot be in your lease, especially if it is a lease for residential property.

[ ] Step 216 -   If you're making or signing a lease, you should still list the ten most important things for your business and make sure those are included. Also, search to make sure you're not giving up something you wouldn't want. If anything is confusing or doesn't seem right, you should hire an attorney.

Conflict of Interest Statements

Every company should have conflict of interest policies, agreed to by the employees, directors, executives and owners of the company. These conflict of interest policies should state what the rule is when one of those involved in the company comes to a point where her decision may positively affect her on a personal level, especially when there is a pecuniary benefit.

Some conflict of interest policies require disclosure, but still allow the person to make the decision. Other policies require that the person abstain from any decision that may result in a positive monetary gain for her personally. It is up to you, taking into account the values of the company, to determine what is the best route for you personally and for the company.

In nonprofit organizations, many times there are specific conflict of interest policies set by state and federal law, so be on the lookout for those if you've started a nonprofit.

[ ] Step 217 -   Write a conflict of interest policy.

[ ] Step 218 -   Add that conflict of interest policy to your employment folder and keep it with your governing documents and company policies.

Doing Everything Safely

More important than having all the legal elements in place is doing everything in a safe manner. This is incredibly important and should be taken to heart.

Once again, more important than having all the legal elements in place is doing everything in a safe manner.

What does this mean? This means you need to be operating in a way to limit your potential liability, don't take unnecessary risks, and fix problems that come up in an effective and nonaggressive manner.

To operate in a way that limits your potential liability, you want to do the research and ask people for help when you need it. A very common mistake is when business owners become numb to problems because they're always around. This allowance of the problem will lead to greater problems.

Social scientists James Q. Wilson and George L. Kelling illustrated a theory about how, in order to lessen crime in a particular neighborhood, all you had to do was fix up the neighborhood. The theory was that since there were already a few broken windows, what's a few more? Not taking care of the smaller problems encourages an atmosphere of escalation. After all the windows are broken, there must be stuff inside to break. By fixing the windows, you're not providing the increased incentive to break the other windows. Similarly, with litter, if there's already a pile of trash on the sidewalk, it appears as though you are doing less harm by adding to the pile.

Ultimately, this principle is called externalities. Externalities are the subsidization of positive or negative effects throughout a larger population. Since you will be less impacted by the spread out harm (in this case risk), you're less likely to care about the negative consequences. If, however, you're the only one doing it, it's going to stand out and you're more likely the one who will get caught and punished. Riots escalate because of this same theory. The more people there are, the less likely that you personally will get caught and punished for your action. Therefore, your mind sees less harm and the perceived benefit outweighs the perceived cost.

In your business, if small problems are allowed to linger, employees, and even you, are more likely to add to the problem because the blame is less attributable to one action or one person. Have you ever been in the position where you have not had enough money to pay your bills and you start spending more? Or pile on more dirty dishes instead of washing them? It's the same concept. You've already encountered many problems and therefore, this one action is not going to affect the outcome as much. If you need $2,000 for rent and you have $2,400, you're going to spend less; however, once you're at $500, it doesn't matter anymore in your mind. What's one more pair of shoes?

You should not take unnecessary risks. Risk is a natural state of being in any business, so it's important to not try to eliminate it, just manage it. Your risk should be minimized by doing research, consulting with your advisors and loved ones, and understanding completely what you're about to do. Furthermore, one key way to ensure that you're minimizing the risk of running your business is to put your mission statement and values where you can reference them every day. Every decision you make should take these into account. If your decision doesn't support these, you're making a bad decision.

You will need to be an educated business manager, knowing as many of the details and expected outcomes of each decision you make. You should also be asking yourself if what you're about to do is going to cause someone to be upset. Usually, an upset person is the catalyst for a lawsuit. Right or wrong, lawsuits end up costing money. If your decision is going to upset someone, determine if there is any way to mitigate the risk of a lawsuit or find ways to make this person less upset.

We cannot please everyone all of the time. However, that does not mean we should not try to lessen how much we upset people, nor should we ever go into a situation looking for a fight. Fights do not benefit anyone. It's cliché to say that everyone loses in a fight, and it's also not true. The lawyers end up winning, and both parties end up losing. You may win the trial, but you've spent many hours and dollars fighting it when you likely could have found a way around it before you got to that point.

There's usually a more attractive business solution to every legal problem. – Joel Touriniemi

The third principle is fixing any problems that come up in an effective and nonaggressive manner. Even if you operate in a way that lessens your liability and you've avoided the unnecessary risks, there will still be problems. Those that handle these problems well set themselves out from the crowd. There are many different ways to deal with a problem, but the best way to deal with it is the way that puts your company in a better position than before there was even a problem.

Problems are opportunities. Every problem comes with choices and how you handle those choices is how the world will see you. It's not about how you act when the waters are calm that makes you a great captain; it's how you weather the storm.

Once a problem presents itself, take a few deep breaths. Even in the case of a fire, you will have two seconds to breathe deeply. This lessens the panic reflex you might be prone to otherwise. Acting without thinking, as you would in a panic situation, is relying on instinct and luck. Typically, our instincts lead us to safety, but not necessarily for our employees or our company. So, take those deep breaths and then visualize the choices you have. Picture each choice and what the expected outcome would be.

Once you've visualized each option and the expected outcome, you want to choose the option that holds truest to your company values and your mission statement. In the case of a fire, you obviously have to act quicker than a lawsuit when you have thirty days to respond. In either circumstance, you will probably feel a fair amount of anxiety by taking the time you need. Suppress that anxiety because it tends to lead you to the wrong decision. Instead, keep telling yourself that you have time. No matter what, you should take the time you need to make the right decision.

If possible, for more difficult problems, you should consult your trusted advisors. Whether you're using your advisory team, a mentor or a professional you work with, it's helpful to get an outside perspective to tell you how they would view your decisions. You will try to justify it in your mind and rationalize it; however, a good advisor will give it to you straight, without any rationalization because it wasn't her decision. We all try to rationalize our decisions and justify our actions after the fact. Your trusted advisors may have already been in similar situations before and can give valuable insight.

The whole principle of doing everything safely revolves a lot around good business sense, but good business sense takes practice to obtain. Nobody is born with it and no one is a natural at it. If you think you are, you may find that you're rationalizing and justifying your decisions. This is one of the main reasons that people are far more likely to succeed on their third company than their first.

[ ] Step 219 -   Think of all the decisions you've made so far and answer whether or not your values and mission statement were the first things considered. If not, go back and redo them, especially your SOP portions.

[ ] Step 220 -   Schedule a time to review all of the documents, policies, procedures, and plans made throughout this book within the next week.

[ ] Step 221 -   Schedule a regular time, at least once per month, to go over your business plan. During this meeting, you should also review your actions to ensure they were the best actions you could have taken under the circumstances, learning where you can.

You now have the foundation for a company ready to grow. All that is left is for you to put your best effort into it and make it succeed. You've already got the tools necessary to grow faster and with fewer issues than most startup companies, so I know you will do great.

On a personal note, I love hearing success stories from other small businesses. I would love to hear from you once you get going. Leave me a review, send me an email, or however you wish to contact me and let me know how your company is doing as you grow.

The Future

If you'd like free bonus content, sneak previews, or access to upcoming guides and resources, please sign up for my mailing list at CheckMarkStartup.com. You can expect infrequent notifications of upcoming publications, tips, and bonus content not otherwise available to my readers.

As I too need to make a living, I cannot spend all my day promoting these books. I need your help with that. If you think this book was useful, please help me get it in the hands of other entrepreneurs so that we can help them grow their businesses.

APPENDIX I – BUSINESS PLAN OUTLINE

1. Executive Summary
2. Values and Mission Statement
3. Goals
4. Products and Services
5. Marketing Plan
   a. Market Analysis
      i. Size
      ii. Competitors
   b. Demographics
   c. Uniqueness
6. Detailed Marketing Plan
7. Pricing
8. Business Needs
9. Financial
10. Team
11. Legal Foundation

APPENDIX II – STARTUP COSTS

Legal Formation   ($400 NC Formation from Law++)

CPA Services   ($1000)

Website   ($750)

Computer   ($500)

Liability Insurance   ($500)

E&O or Professional Liability Insurance   ($1500)

Leased Space   ($12,000)

Legal Services   ($2,000)

  Contracts

  General Guidance

  Governing Document

  Stock Agreements

Accounting Software   ($300)

Marketing Expenses   ($4000)

APPENDIX III – FUNDING SOURCE MILESTONES

Bank Loan

Milestone 1. Create a list of 5 local banks, 5 national banks, and 2 internet banks.

Milestone 2. Call or visit each bank to ask (and write down):

    a. Do you provide startup business loans or similar service?

        i. If not, can you recommend someone who does?

    b. Do you require a cosigner on the loan?

    c. What interest rate would I get on the loan?

    d. How long is the payment term?

    e. What fees are there on the loan? Origination fee?

    f. Is there any prepayment penalty?

    g. Is there a grace period before I must start making payments?

    h. Do you have any programs that could help us in case we have a downturn month?

Milestone 3. Based on the information gathered and what's important to me, which bank should I choose?

Milestone 4. Apply for the loan.

Milestone 5. Loan Closing.

Investor

Milestone 1.   Get a valuation of the company.

Milestone 2.   Calculate percent willing to give up based on value and how much investment is needed.

    a. Investment/valuation.

Milestone 3.   Make a list of as many investors in the area I can find.

Milestone 4.   Research each investor to determine what types of companies they invest in and what requirements they typically include.

    a. Look for information on their websites and LinkedIn profiles.

    b. Call companies they've invested in.

    c. Don't call them yet.

Milestone 5.   Eliminate any investors that don't invest in your area or that have restrictions that you are not willing to follow.

Milestone 6.   Create a pitch deck.

Milestone 7.   Create a 30 second, 1 minute, 3 minute, 5 minute and 15 minute pitch.

Milestone 8.   Get a lawyer to advise on seeking investment.

Milestone 9.   Either reach out directly or actively seek an introduction to the investors remaining in the list for the purpose of getting investment.

Milestone 10.   Accept or reject any offers received.

Milestone 11.   Get lawyer to draft investment documents.

APPENDIX IV – SAMPLE SKILLS

My Skills

Production	Expansion

• Web Development
   o Javascript
   o PHP
   o .Net
   o HTML
   o CSS
   o Java
• Social Media Platform Development
   o Facebook API
   o Twitter API
   o LinkedIn API
	• Social Media Marketing
	   o Facebook
	   o Twitter
	   o LinkedIn
	   o Google+
	• Networking
	• Marketing Plan

Protection	**Administrative**
• Strategic Planning	• Word Processing • Document Drafting • Proposal Writing

Company's Needed Skills

Production	**Expansion**

• Web Development
  ○ Javascript
  ○ PHP
  ○ .Net
  ○ HTML
  ○ CSS
  ○ Java
• Social Media Platform Development
  ○ Facebook API
  ○ Twitter API
  ○ LinkedIn API
  ○ Pinterest
  ○ Google+
  ○ Instagram
  ○ MySpace
	• Social Media Marketing
	  ○ Facebook
	  ○ Twitter
	  ○ LinkedIn
	  ○ Google+
	  ○ Pinterest
	  ○ Instagram
	• Networking
	• Marketing Plan
	• Print Materials
	  ○ Pamphlets
	  ○ Brochures
	• Website
	• Events
	• Speaking Engagements

Protection	**Administrative**

• Legal
  ○ Business Structure
  ○ Operating Agreement
  ○ Customer Contracts
  ○ Service Provider Contracts
  ○ Employee Contracts
  ○ Equity Agreements
• Insurance
  ○ Key Person Insurance
  ○ Life Insurance
  ○ General Business Insurance
  ○ Other
	• Bookkeeping
	• Document Drafting
	• Emailing
	• Scheduling
	• Client Database Management
	• Workflow management
	• Proposal Writing
	• Taxes

APPENDIX V – SAMPLE LETTER TO FAMILY AND FRIENDS

Dear friend:

In the upcoming months, I am going to be starting my own business making software for schools throughout the United States. I'm doing this because I'm passionate about education and believe that I can make a software solution that uniquely addresses the needs of school systems in an impactful way. I don't know what my future may hold for me going down this path, but I am certain this is what I need to be doing with my life right now.

I'm writing this letter to you because I consider you one of my closest friends. I wanted to let you know that this journey is important to me, but it will also likely be stressful and very hard at times. I know that I will likely reach out to you often to grab a drink and just vent about my day, and I am very appreciative if you would be there for me. You've always been there for me in the past, as I will always be available for you when you need me.

What I could definitely use from you is your continued love and support, as well as to remind me why I'm doing this when things look down. Be sure to remind me to be nice to my mom as well!

Love you and thank you,

Richard Bobholz

ABOUT THE AUTHOR

Richard Bobholz is an award-winning attorney, speaker, business owner, teacher, and dedicated community member. He is the author of several other books in the business and science fiction genres, focusing his more recent publications on business, legal, and computer programming. Beyond helping his community through these resources, Richard dedicates a significant amount of his time to providing community service and pro bono legal services to the less fortunate in his community.

Richard enjoys running, backpacking, computer programming, writing, and spending time with family and friends.

Richard obtained his Bachelor's Degree in Economics at Michigan Technological University and his Juris Doctorate from the Kline School of Law at Drexel University.

Richard currently practices at Law Plus Plus, a revolutionary and award-winning law firm that is dedicated to making the legal system easier, enacting positive change in the community, and constantly improving how they operate and the effect they have on their clients' lives and in their profession. With this mission and his genuine approach to the practice of law, he is able to help small businesses, nonprofits, and social entrepreneurs protect themselves and develop their businesses in a deliberate and systematic manner.

In 2015, Law Plus Plus was recognized by the American Bar Association for their contribution to pro bono services, taking second place nationwide for their commitment, and in 2016, Law Plus Plus became the first law firm in North Carolina to become B Corporation Certified.

Beyond those accomplishments, the attorneys at Law Plus Plus also contribute hundreds of hours every year toward community service through programs like Habitat for Humanity, Clean Jordan Lake, the Food Bank, Activate Good and so many more.

Richard also sits on the Board of Trustees for Activate Good, an amazing organization that promotes and pairs volunteers with causes, creating a multiplier effect in the community. The organization not only supports these nonprofits, but also inspires the next generation of leaders through their Activate Schools program and gives the resources needed to get businesses involved in coordinated days of service for their employees.

www.ingramcontent.com/pod-product-compliance
Lightning Source LLC
Chambersburg PA
CBHW070502200326
41519CB00013B/2683